Competitive Edge
through
Credit Management

Competitive Edge
through
Credit Management

Michael O'Sullivan

ADDISON-WESLEY PUBLISHING COMPANY

Wokingham, England • Reading, Massachusetts • Menlo Park,
California • New York • Don Mills, Ontario • Amsterdam
Bonn • Sydney • Singapore • Tokyo • Madrid • San Juan
Milan • Paris • Mexico City • Seoul • Taipei

Many of the designations used by manufacturers and sellers to distinguish
their products are claimed as trademarks. Addison-Wesley has made every
attempt to supply trademark information about manufacturers and their
products mentioned in this book.

Cover designed by Designers & Partners of Oxford and
printed by The Riverside Printing Co. (Reading) Ltd.
Typeset by Colset Private Limited, Singapore.
Printed in Great Britain by T.J. Press (Padstow) Ltd, Cornwall.

First printed 1992.

ISBN: 0 201 56881 0

British Library Cataloguing in Publication Data

A catalogue record for this book is available from the British Library.

recycled paper

Preface

WHAT THIS BOOK IS ABOUT

The aim of this book is to boost company profitability by gaining sustainable competitive advantage through more effective use of credit management and customer information. The book sets out to do three things:

(1) To demonstrate how senior management can use the credit department to close the gap between corporate intent and operational delivery – without incurring any extra costs.

(2) To heighten individual awareness by exposing company people to customer information on how each company function can contribute to:

    (a) better customer service;
    (b) improvement in the quality of the activity;
    (c) overall company performance.

(3) To provide a practical customer-orientated training manual on how to set up and operate a credit department at any level.

WHO THIS BOOK IS FOR

- Senior management
- Managers who allow credit
- Credit staff

THE FLAVOUR OF CREDIT MANAGEMENT

Most of the 850 000 companies in the United Kingdom offer credit as a way of selling their products.

It works simply. You let customers have your goods and they promise to pay you. If, for example, you are a construction equipment manufacturer you wait an average 63 days for your customers to pay you.

Construction equipment manufacturers make an average 5.5% profit annually. So if you are the average and you are allowing 63 days' credit, this costs 2.76% of your annual sales in bank interest. This is equivalent to half your company's profitability.

And there is another feature to think about. According to the Institute of Credit Management one-third of the assets of British business are tied up in trade debts (credit allowed). This means that other people control one-third of your assets.

THE FLAVOUR OF CUSTOMER INFORMATION

Customers will tell you all that you want to know about them – but only if you listen. Listening not only safeguards these assets of yours that they hold but also truly assures your future – because they will actually tell you what they want you to do for them.

Your success will depend on the degree to which you actively listen to customers and respond to their needs.

Mike O'Sullivan
Peterborough, July 1991

For simplicity, the pronoun 'he' is used to relate to both male and female throughout the book.

Contents

| Contents |

PART I

Sustainable Competitive Advantage through Credit Management

The Concept

Companies spend much time and effort sorting out processes and procedures to get information out to customers. Examples are advertising and invoices. Yet some companies fail to listen actively when customers respond.

The concept is simple enough. It is to capture information with the aim of orientating all company people to respond to customers immediately. The credit department is best placed to take on the task of organizing this integrated operational link-up.

Most people would say that credit management is all about collecting customers' money. Traditionally true, but this is changing. Its role is expanding.

1.1 Operations link

Credit management is the one link in the routine day-to-day operations of a company that stays with the sale from its beginning through to its conclusion in payment. Throughout this time it sees what is, in effect, the entire commercial transaction. It encounters reactions from internal sources as far apart as marketing and production and is in constant contact with the customer (or should be). The sheer volume of information flowing in and out of its clutches can be astonishing. Most of this is customer information. And most of it is lost.

Your corporate culture determines the weight you give to customer opinion, as against other forms of measuring how you are doing. When you look through your monthly company report is there any indication in it of how your customers feel about the company? Do your management team, in the main, echo customer worries or do they concentrate instead on internally generated financial data? What is important to you?

There are certain aspects about customer information that make it the most valuable information in the business. It is given willingly. It is concise. It is about the future. And, more important than any other single source, it expresses exactly what customers want. The credit department can get this information.

It can do much better than this. It can present the information to any company department in the way the department wants it. Remarkably, supplying this information actually reduces the work of the credit department.

1.2 Credit skills

The skills needed to deliver just the basics of good cash collection are more complex than you think. To do well you need to be an above average communicator – you have to sell yourself to customers, juggle the sales and finance interests and have the listening capacity of an agony aunt in order to hear customers' complaints. You must deliver figures close to the sales figures of the previous month and on top of this you have to appear honest and fair. About 80% of the time will be spent talking to customers. On-the-spot decisions affecting future trading of the company become a way of life.

It is, therefore, essential to have well trained people in this crucial department. Some of this book is in the form of a training manual. So for the busy executive wanting a second opinion on what the credit people are up to, or should be up to, this book can act as a quick reference. The concept draws on the skills that credit people acquire, and explores how they can best be used for the benefit of the company.

1.3 Change

The UK is a cautious, financial-management-led business environment. A 'don't take risks' rather than a 'try anything once' approach. Mistakes are solidly punished and those who make them put down. Yet it's a well-known fact that 9 out of 10 ventures fail. People who don't take chances can nonetheless find themselves at the top. A perpetual no-risk policy can prevail. A market-geared credit philosophy can change this negative approach.

Say you were contemplating change. Change is an emotive subject. You would have to be fairly certain that the effort you were going to put in was going to be worth it. You might start by creating the atmosphere to allow a review of your current approach to managing the business. This would need delicate handling. Your words and motives would be suspected. And you would need the full cooperation of the workforce.

The workforce may not feel inclined to take the benefit of your advice on what is best for the company. But with the exception of the monopolistic enterprise, the workforce will listen to the advice of customers. Therefore, any review or appraisal of your business would be best served by being dominated by customer references. The long-term answer would then appear to be, to stay close to the customers. The credit department is in constant touch with customers' advice, which is constantly changing. Therefore, there is a strong element of change in the information held by credit. It is the use of this information that can create the atmosphere for change. Change is automatically built into the information flow of the credit department.

1.4 Summary

- The concept links customers with internal company processes. Processes become value added. Individual horizons are broadened. Tight operational links encourage company teamwork. The company is able to change with the market, even lead it.

The Discussion

The approach here is to try at all times to focus attention on the customers. In every organization the extent to which customers are given priority will determine the quality of service these customers receive.

The drive for quality, if it is to stand any chance of success, must be led by the chief executive. It must be fully supported by the entire workforce. It would help to have the words 'quality' and 'customers' in the main company message. This would not only establish the company's intention in the general market-place but also act as a constant reminder to the workforce of what is expected of them. To translate good intentions into good quality operations requires the will and determination of everyone in monitoring the service, from the chief executive down to the first-level employee. The credit department is ideally situated to help do just this.

If it hasn't crossed your mind before, credit management's cash collection effort is at the end of your whole company process. This is where customers complain about products and services – sometimes *without* their cheque books in front of them. Most of what they say, a tremendous source of feedback on customer satisfaction levels, is lost forever. And yet here in these complaints lie the future answers to your marketing strategy.

The information is unsolicited, given willingly and should therefore be more accurate than the kind of general marketing information most companies use. It is also free.

This information is available for collection by the credit department every day. What you get from it and how you use it will depend on your approach to credit management.

2.1 The basics

Your own set of circumstances will influence your attitude to business in general and the workplace in particular.

With which of the following set of values would you find most sympathy?

A	B	C	D
Customers	Management	Shareholders	Employees
Employees	Shareholders	Management	Customers
Shareholders	Employees	Customers	Management
Management	Customers	Employees	Shareholders

The urgent need to satisfy customers' wants is absent far too often. In some management circles satisfying the customer is treated only as a concept. By the time this message filters down to the first-level employee, whose main task might be dealing with customers, the internal signals can become confusing. This confusion is transmitted to customers in contact with the company.

However, management may be totally unaware of what is happening. The marketing slogans become *only* slogans. The message is lost somewhere between marvellous intent and practical management inability to deliver.

Take some everyday examples of corporate messages not getting through:

- *Supermarkets* Products are elaborately packaged to gain attention. Such detail is surely missed by the check-out staff who can't wait to get the customer out, making full use of the moving belt to crush the treasured packages, if customers are not fast packers.

- *Town councils* One town council is so overworked that the answerphone is on during office hours.

- *Construction companies* They build motorways and then block large sections off even though they are not working.

- *Internal company telephone extensions* Phones are left to ring.

- *Manufacturers* Some sell electric products without a plug.
- *Lorry and van drivers* Some use their company vehicles to push other motorists off the road.
- *Sportsmen* They sometimes cheat with the 'professional foul'.
- *TV news interviewers* They sometimes seem more interested in the numbers killed or maimed, and how badly injured.

These examples sometimes result in carelessness in kind; no cooperation with officials; letting off steam, which can be dangerous on the roads; customers going elsewhere for a better service; and TV currently losing viewers. Coupled with this is the general acceptance that UK companies can also sell 'seconds'. We become a 'seconds' society.

2.2 The size of the involvement

Table 2.1 shows the average number of days the industry sectors involved in building houses took to collect their money during the year 1988/89.

In credit jargon the number of days is called days' sales outstanding (or DSO). They are also sometimes called debtor days or the credit period.

There are numerous reasons why all these industry sectors allow credit to the extent that they do. Some of these reasons are weak but understandable. There is almost a sense of an unofficial traditional pecking order when comparing the major and intermediate building and civil engineering sectors. Roofing contractors allow customers more time to pay than window manufacturers.

At some levels of process the construction industry is easy to enter and exit. If, to the outsider, the industry of house building looks difficult to understand this is because, as in the ordinary average building site it sometimes resembles, the emphasis is always changing. Sometimes it is not clear just by looking at a site when the work of one trade is finished. This is

Table 2.1 Average number of days the industry sectors involved in house building took to collect their money in 1988/89.

Building materials industry
Brick and tile manufacturers 94
Building insulation 74
Construction equipment manufacturers 63
Construction steelwork manufacturers 63
Joinery manufacturers 56
Pre-cast concrete manufacturers 69
Process plant manufacturers 85
Window manufacturers 52
Ready mixed concrete and aggregates 64

Construction industry
Builders' merchants 65
Building and civil engineering contractors
  Major 28
  Intermediate 41
House builders 18
Construction equipment distributors 50
Plant hire processes 71
Plant contractors 54
Roofing contractors 72

Others
Electrical contractors 67
Electrical installation manufacturers 69
Electrical wholesalers 71
Lighting equipment manufacturers 67
Heating and ventilating equipment manufacturers 78
Heating and ventilating contractors 45
Insulation contractors 80
Painting and decorating contractors 49
Steel producers 79
Timber (importers) 63

Carpet manufacturers 51
Kitchen and bathroom furniture manufacturers 45
Contract furniture 58

Estate agents 57

Source: *Industrial Performance Analysis 1988/89*, published by ICC Publications.

mainly because they do not tidy up after they have completed their work. It is this kind of situation that employs an army of people in the industry busily trying to sort out unfinished work from finished work. It may even appear that there are more people sorting out problems than there are people creating them.

Consider for a moment the people who dig up the roads. The normal practice is that one service comes along to do some repair work. They burst a water pipe. Then the water people come along and tap in unintentionally to the electricity supply. The electricity people knock a gas pipe. And so it goes on. This is because no one at the town hall knows where all the various services are. Also nowadays the main services use subcontractors who seem to change the people on the one stretch of road every few days and just when they have got to know where all the other services are.

On a day-to-day basis the more successful organizations, whether five-people businesses or multinationals, sound and feel successful because they listen to both the employee and the customer. They become more flexible; they relate better to each other and to customers; and they are more helpful. They are also more skilled and better trained. Their companies are better organized and better managed.

Some companies have not yet discovered the art of good listening. Take the following example.

> I once attended a gathering of small companies that were having trouble collecting their debts. Their stated objective was to reverse this situation quickly.
>
> They decided the best way to do this was to form an association that would invite experts to advise them. As an initial step this meeting was set up and I was invited to talk to them on cash collection.
>
> As the meeting progressed it became apparent that they had already previously assumed that the expert advice would readily be available and that all would benefit, i.e. the experts and their members.
>
> The members then turned their attention to the way the association would be formed. The make-up of its governing body, if memory serves me well, was going to be a limited company with some of the personnel present as its directors. Many of the ideas were already on paper before the meeting started. These included

such details as the future office locations and how they would be managed. Much time was spent on trying to categorize both the future membership from the point of view of their interest in the services and the charges which this interest might carry in member-ship fees. In fact it transpired that the chargeable fees element was taking over as the main reason for the setting up of the association. In the end it transpired I was expected to pay an initial fee too, as I would be making money out of their members who would seek my advice.

What they failed to grasp was that I had no trouble collecting money and by definition would not therefore have any reason to join the association. In fact they had not really addressed the problem of how I would be paid for any advice I would give. The significance of this was not lost on me. But if I, as an expert, could not see how I was going to get paid, I would feel reasonably reluc-tant to spend any time on the association's work (as presumably would any other expert who might be called in). It follows that without advisers they might have some difficulty meeting their first objective.

Here was a group whose only folly was to lose sight of the customers, in this case themselves.

2.3 All that glitters

A sale is not a sale until the money is collected.

Some organizations are sales orientated. That is, they concen-trate their efforts on sales. This requires the rest of the organiza-tion to be as fast as salespeople in the services they supply. This may not always be so. Take this example.

I was called in by the MD of one highly successful company in the computer field to look at the cash collection problem.

The company personnel were basically selling all day on the telephone. They did not spend enough time on the buying and supply side of the business.

The result was that the supply line became sluggish. Fulfilling the detail on any unusual order caused complications and pro-blems. Much of the business at this time catered for the unusual order. Customers who received a poor service reflected their disapproval, sometimes by taking longer to pay their accounts. This, of course, affected the cash collection. Because of the delay in supplying the customers with products, other complications were beginning to set in.

The installation manager's programme became difficult to schedule. He would arrange to install systems on particular days – maybe weeks in advance – only to cancel because the equipment was not delivered on time. Likewise, the trainer had some post-ponements. His schedule sometimes revolved around the installa-tion of the machines. Where there were multiple orders for several sites by one customer, from several suppliers, some would arrive, others would not. The customer was having to check around the offices. This was not good news.

However, looking at the positive side, the problems were identified and the MD was able to take appropriate action before any major disasters materialized. A reduction in DSO followed.

An effective credit management function would have dis-covered the company's shortcomings at an early date and would have been able to advise on appropriate action.

2.4 The quality of the activity

It isn't enough to formulate a good marketing strategy and to advertise the company's intentions to the market, without explaining to the workforce what is expected of them to deliver the strategy targets.

Most company departments get into a daily routine. Such routines evolve by having to cope with the work that arrives each day. The work schedule is usually planned to cope with the workload. But is anyone monitoring the quality of the work? Is anyone monitoring the reasons for the work? And is the work relevant or necessary to the business? Some departments can get so bogged down with the procedures and practices that they lose sight of why they are operating in the way that they are. Take the following example.

I know of a director of a large multinational whose secretary had to type five copies of his letters and memos.

These were all different colours, pink, yellow, grey, blue and beige, so that it reminded him who they were for. When she sometimes got them in the wrong order there was hell to pay. The kind of administration network that went into this daily but simple task would normally have most secretaries in dire straits. But she had in fact learned to take it from the present director's predecessor.

It is sometimes very difficult to question practices and procedures. Normally, when joining a company, incoming employees will ask questions in all innocence. They will have experienced good and bad practices previously. They will bring some of each with them. They are being hired because of what they may be able to do.

Normally an incoming employee will be shown the ropes by the employee who is leaving. In four or five weeks the new employee may start to complete tasks in another way, contrary to company procedure. This may turn out to be a better way of doing things. However, it may lead to mistakes being made by the employee. If the company does not accept change, the new employee may have to accept the company's way of doing things whether it is right or wrong. It seems a shame that the new employee cannot contribute anything personal. Yet, this is so in the majority of cases.

Sometimes, specific strategies are planned, marketed to the public or industry by professionals, closely monitored by the board for signs of progress, while at the same time the operational reins are left to chance. Chance because no one has explained to the workforce the basis of the new strategy, the current national TV advertising campaign and their role in it.

There are everyday examples of public image building with little or no workforce involvement or interest in the outcome. You just have to look at the national utilities, the transport systems, and the local authorities to get some idea of the depth of the problem. Setting up a mechanism where railway station staff, gas fitters and rubbish collectors can feel confident that management will listen to their ideas encourages them to come up with ideas. In fact none of these organizations can even dream of success without the commitment of the workforce. Impartial monitoring systems are necessary to get the ideas out into the open and achieve the best results. However, everyday examples of internal communication breakdown abound.

In the 'more commercial' field this gap between management intent and operational delivery could arise quite naturally without a second thought. Take a producer of chocolates. You know how the advertisement goes. Man jumps out of helicopter, swims snake-infested channel, fights off wolves, to deliver chocolates. And here you are trying to order chocolates, waiting five minutes for the company's switchboard to answer.

How far do these seemingly unimportant junior tasks reflect senior managers' thinking? Does any monitoring process link the two? How easy are they to spot? Take this example.

> On a visit to a nationally known company in the computer industry the scene that greeted me as I walked through the entrance was like something out of a John Cleese training film.
>
> There were lots of people walking to and fro on different levels clutching pieces of paper. There was a keen sense of fashionable dress and an air of pleasant activity.
>
> However, there did not seem to be any sense of purpose. For all the activity nothing much seemed to be getting done. No one seemed to be working. The receptionist was absent.
>
> During my visit it was mentioned that the company had just secured an overseas order which would double its turnover.
>
> The credit department reflected the other processes I was able to observe. There was nobody there.
>
> The company folded up a few months later. How could it deliver its marketing intention, if no one was there?
>
> An effective credit department would have been able to spot the signs well in advance.

2.5 Change

Many people will have gone through change in the way their organization operates. It is surprising what little planning is put into the process of change.

Change can mean different things to different people. A redesign of the reception area might change layout, colour, accessibility or comfort. This might greatly impress visitors, make security more difficult to operate, save on maintenance costs and create a sense of pride in the receptionist.

A change in the computer system is nowadays the most common change that affects a credit department. Having selected a system from the 250 or so available the next task is to change over systems. There are two ways of doing this: either run the current and new systems together in parallel, gradually moving to the new system, or load all the current information into the new system at one go and hope for the best. Each has its merits. And it is hard work whichever route you choose.

The disruption caused by a change in computer system is stressful for credit staff at the best of times. There are agonizing waits after data is loaded and before the results are known. Will the accounts balance? Is the information on each account correct? Can we go home without doing overtime just one night? Do we really look like zombies? But after the initial couple of weeks of getting to grips with a new system, management is inclined to ignore the rest of the moaning that accompanies such change. A change may take two to three months. But it could take a year before everyone is back to normal.

In the normal course of events change is something the credit department experiences each day. If customers don't like the service they change to a competitor. What the credit department can do is to deliver the change the customer wants so that the business relationship stays on course.

But the desire for change must be universal throughout the company. The strategy must be clear. Everyone must get involved. Everyone must be listened to. Change must be well planned. If mistakes are made they must be acknowledged and corrected. If you show people that you aim to get it right they will be more inclined to believe you. The show must go on. Someone once said that all business should be show business.

A change in the computer system will affect users intensely. Their fears have to be understood and catered for. The benefits need to be fully explained.

Any change in systems will bring the workforce into contact with the companies selling the systems. The workforce will have to cope with new jargon. New schedules will be put into operation because of the initial extra workload in effecting the change.

It is a great advantage to a credit department to reconcile the accounts before a change in computer system. This will make for less work in the long run. Of course, the best method of reconciling the accounts is to collect the amounts owing. Perhaps a planned extra effort before the changes might save nail-biting later. There will be lots of overtime devoted to the changeover. Dramatic errors may occur. I remember once wiping off two days' work and having to go down on hands and knees to the staff to ask forgiveness.

> There was the case where the director chairing the meetings on an intended new computer system did not think it was a good idea to take minutes of the meetings.
> After some months there developed a sense of unreality and dread. No one was certain of fully understanding the terminology that was being used. There were even times when those present were confidently using terms and phrases that were quite meaningless. Each new system that was discussed brought some new words into the general arena. But meetings really started getting out of hand when people used the same simple everyday words to mean entirely different things. By this time the credit manager had stopped attending the meetings.
> When the implications became obvious the director changed his mind about taking notes. However, by this time many had left the company out of frustration.
> The show was not a resounding success.
> Those same employees with mixed feelings about the value to the company of the work they did, were obliged to talk each day to customers in a confident, knowledgeable and friendly manner, while collecting cash. The stress placed on the employees far outweighed their rewards for doing their work. It was completely unnecessary and could have been avoided by good planning. Yet they carried on with the show.
> More applause for the troopers.

Some people don't like change because it is different. Others don't like change because they are happy the way things are. Yet others can't see the value in a particular change. The people who don't like change might not like their current way of doing things either.

Change may not even be the answer. The credit department

can deliver change without it being detected as change. Continuing change, or built-in change hardly feels like change at all. You could call it customer advice.

What you can get from your customers is information which will concisely point out what you are doing wrong and perhaps how you can put it right. On a small scale it might be advice about the best time to deliver goods, or a possible solution to a particular problem with a product. In getting them involved in your processes and you in theirs (the more involved the more they will come back) you will also learn from them what they want in the future.

The concept is simple enough. The process is simple. The customers love to get involved. And your workforce can relate much more to customers than to company monthly financial reports. The systems can be as simple or sophisticated as you want them to be. There is a suggested system in Chapter 10.

2.6 The company culture

The company culture as it may affect credit management is shown in Table 2.2.

Table 2.2 Company culture and credit management.

Culture	Language
Highly motivated Market led	Plan, market, customer targets, manage, monitor
Tightly controlled Finance led	Control, discounts, queries, chase, terms and conditions
Losing control Crisis led	Demand, complaints, bad debts, solicitors
Lost control Headless	Courts, insolvency, winding up, execution

MARKETING LED CREDIT MANAGEMENT

At the very forefront of marketing led credit management is removal of the credit function from under the wing of finance to have it report direct to the sales director.

Such a company structure could have the credit manager deputizing for the sales director in his absence. The effect of this structure in the sales department is to put a light financial restraint on the salespeople in the director's absence. In the normal course of events the credit manager would be on a par with the sales manager. The balance of the company's operation emphasis is therefore marketing orientated.

This kind of arrangement puts pressure on the credit department to get to know the market better. It is then led by market knowledge. This is more relevant than financial constraints which tend to be more concerned with concise reconciliation of figures. Where cash collection is marketing led the need to reconcile becomes less necessary. This is because more emphasis is placed on up-front customer contact which results in earlier collection targeting. Hence there are fewer unsolved queries and less cash outstanding on the accounts to reconcile. Customers' payables departments are kept happy with clean statements.

Generally, companies with marketing led credit management tend to be better at communicating externally. Attention to detail tends to be more customer friendly. The switchboard is answered quickly. The internal phones are picked up faster. Phone calls are returned. Customers are more inclined to extend their confidences to a friendly company. These confidences will give the 'easy-to-contact' company a competitive advantage.

In such a marketing led company there would be a system of passing on customers' comments to the relevant departments. These would be analysed periodically. The analysis and results would be fed into the mainstream company reporting systems and any new or better way for doing things discussed in open forum. Where problems occurred, project teams drawn from different departments would be picked to find solutions and disbanded when they found the solutions. Good interdepartmental relations would be maintained.

A typical effect this might have on the credit manager might be for him to visit a customer while the customer's account was entirely up to date. While there, the credit manager might possibly see other aspects of the customer's operations outside the payables department. This information could become invaluable in solving some later problem.

Keeping the workforce tuned in to the customers is about the best training they can get.

FINANCE LED CREDIT MANAGEMENT

Practically all UK companies' credit departments report to a finance manager. Sometimes this reporting manager is the finance director and sometimes a middle manager. The further away from the board the credit manager sits the more difficult his task becomes.

The training of the finance manager is crucial to the marketing and sales departments and to the credit department. A finance manager with broad experience, as against one with only specialized knowledge of accounting functions, is more likely to be sympathetic to customer led philosophy. But whereas the marketing and salespeople have their own champions, i.e. directors, to forward their causes, the credit department, which is customer orientated by nature, is firmly under the control of financial constraints.

These restraints can sometimes feature more procedural work than is good for the business. Take the following example.

> You never win an argument with a customer. A put-down customer will go elsewhere.
>
> The buyer of a major high street chain arranged a meeting with a sales director and credit manager of a perfume manufacturer, with a view to sorting out delays in paying the accounts.
>
> They met at the buyer's office in central London. The meeting proved to be a total success. The buyer arranged a further meeting between the credit manager and his own purchase ledger manager to work out a few minor details.
>
> The finance director of the perfume manufacturer, who had apparently been kept in the picture, decided at this time to reply to an old letter from the customer. In his letter he advised the customer of the terms of payment and asked for them to be strictly adhered to in future. The letter was addressed to someone who

was not only junior to the purchase manager but who had left the company. Its tone was not sympathetic to the recently improved business climate created by the meeting. The main point that the letter made had already been accepted by the customer.

The purchase ledger manager advised that he never received the letter. He cancelled the scheduled meeting with a plausible excuse. The meeting never took place and the account remained in the state it was in before the meeting with the buyer.

THE TWO-YEAR MANAGER

A feature of some multinationals is the two-year manager. This is someone who is doing the rounds of the various company divisions, taking on more at each step or moving sideways to gain more experience.

A feature of their term of office is to make a mark in each job they do. This means change. Change must be handled carefully. However, time is not on their side. They are under pressure to do well. Any mistakes they make can be corrected by the next manager who takes their place. If they hit lucky they make their mark.

Managing people is not normally one of their better traits. People who report to them become good at adapting to the new managers at the expense of other aspects of their work.

A two-year manager is an expert on the internal company mechanisms, some of which will be favoured more than others. The favoured ones will get promoted more openly, sometimes irrespective of their value. This can have a demoralizing effect on all those involved. The two-year manager is not known to be hot on consulting before taking the plunge down particular routes.

However, a marketing led company is customer orientated. Therefore, the internal systems are dictated by customers' needs. They are driven by outside forces, perhaps only relevant to the particular industry sector in which the two-year manager has now entered. Change is constant and difficult even for those in the industry to stay with. It will seem more difficult for any one person to effect major change. Therefore, the company is much more easily able to absorb any tearaway manager whose ideas are not in keeping with customers' needs.

FROM PUBLIC SECTOR TO PRIVATE SECTOR

An organization that does not put customers first in everything it does, must be more interested in itself. This always shows. Such organizations will be more interested in company culture, management structures, controls and procedures.

A recent report on cultural change of organizations moving out of the public sector into the private sector shows that customer service is not the most important priority for chief executives.

The report, *Privatisation – Implications for Cultural Change*, by management consultants United Research, supported by the

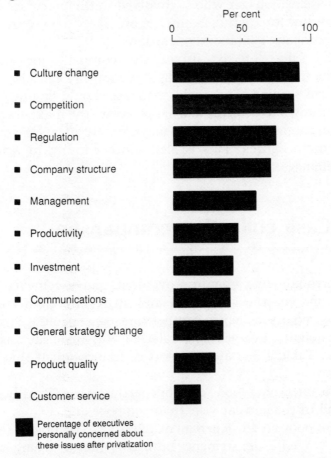

Figure 2.1 Concerns of chief executives. (*Source*: United Research and London Business School.)

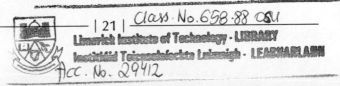

Centre for Business Strategy at The London Business School, summarizes the views of chief executives of 42 organizations employing over 1 million people.

Figure 2.1 shows the concerns of chief executives.

2.7 Sales and cashflow forecasts

Jan Carlzon, Chief Executive of SAS airlines, says that 'an individual without information cannot take responsibility; an individual with information cannot help but take responsibility'.

A credit manager who is involved in the processes of sales and cashflow forecasting is much more likely to take an interest in the company's financial operations.

The sales forecast drives the company forward. The cashflow forecast keeps it going. No company can lose sight of either and survive. The credit manager should be one of those who sits down to determine what goes into the make-up of these two operational tools, since his work greatly affects the outcome of the main figures. This is also another forum in which the credit manager can air views.

2.8 Cash collection comparison

It is worth knowing what improvements can be achieved in cash collection. For the successful and struggling credit manager alike, comparisons with competitors can encourage them to greater heights. Everything is relative. Any little success is still success. Table 2.3 shows the sort of improvement that can be achieved.

The effective ('good') credit department has £2 million more to spend in the current year than the poor one.

The poor credit department loses £276,000 more than the effective credit department in bank interest charges. This amounts to 1.6% of turnover.

An example of how cash collection can affect cashflow is

Table 2.3 Cash collection comparison. Winners and losers with turnover of £17 million and bank interest rate 16%.

	DSO	Cash tied up (£)	Bank interest (£)	Total cash tied up (£)	Difference in cashflow (£)
Good	43	2,003,000	320,000	2,323,000	
Average	65	3,027,000	484,000	3,511,000	1,188,000
Poor	80	3,726,000	596,000	4,322,000	1,999,000

shown in Table 2.4. The example shows an improvement in cash collection of 10 days. It is a sobering thought to reflect that 62 days' credit is equal to 19.5% of annual turnover; 10 days credit improvement is equal to 3.1% of annual turnover.

Table 2.4 Cashflow improvement through cash collection.

Annual turnover (£)	Credit period days	Cost of credit (15% bank interest) (£)	Cash tied up (£)	Total cash tied up (£)
35,000,000	62	892,000	5,945,000	6,837,000
35,000,000	52	748,000	4,986,000	5,734,000
Improvement	10	144,000	959,000	1,103,000

Improvement in cashflow in first year   £1,103,000
Saving in each successive year   £144,000

2.9 Summary

- The culture of the company is led by the chief executive and the board.

- This lead affects the day-to-day operations routine of each member of the workforce. Their day is spent in communication with customers and company people. Cementing relationships with customers is crucial to company success. Integrating company people is also crucial. More attention to the detail of what the customers want and how to get it for them could give you the edge on the competition.

- The credit department is in a unique position to be able to formulate an accurate picture of what customers want and therefore how the company can respond.

- The customers also take care of the bottom line (see Table 2.4).

- The approach is all important.

What some Chief Executives say about Credit Management

This chapter contains the comments of 10 chief executives and chairmen, recorded during personal interviews, on the role and importance of credit management in their companies.

The choice of industrial sector demonstrates the different aspects of each sector and the attitudes to credit management, customer service, customer information and quality control which are all linked.

The interviews, which appear in the order they were conducted, were held after the rest of the book was written.

3.1 Interview 1

Steve Jolliffe of Business Efficiency Monitoring Ltd (BEM), specialists in customer service assessment, says that good cash collection is the key to the success of his business. And it is becoming more important, as his business is growing fast, doubling each year. He measures his debts in debtor days. He aims to collect debts within 40 days, but needs the money within 60 days, otherwise the pressure on his business by borrowing finance is enormous.

He has no one dedicated credit person, but thinks this might be a realistic alternative to his present arrangements. Currently, a fellow director has the task of coordinating billing and cash collection. The credit terms that normally apply are those negotiated at the time the contract is drawn up. Good negotiation skills are important. Steve adds, 'It's all about having the right relationship with clients'.

Steve would not entertain factoring or invoice discounting because this would lose the close relationship he has with clients. Everything depends on the person-to-person contact. If this is good, his invoice will be marked for early payment when it is received.

When the business first started he was a bit slow to insist on payment terms. However, as its reputation increased, so did his attention to payment details. He considers it strategically important to pay attention to payment terms. To reinforce this in his consultancy, Steve is considering a bonus scheme which, instead of being based on the work completion date, would be based on the date when payment was received.

Steve has more respect and higher regard for a supplier who combines a good customer service approach with requests for payment – provided the manner is professional. He feels that such an approach improves the business relationship: 'These kinds of companies tend to be well managed and not ones that just allow things to happen.'

Steve would expect a dedicated credit and collection person to do the job for about two years before further career development. But further career development would be a definite consideration.

3.2 Interview 2

Francis Holford of Rudolf Wolff, a prominent member of the London Metal Exchange, sums up his credit operation: 'In our business credit is very much a daily thing. Although we have very good systems, daily vigilance is most important. A successful credit operation is vital.'

His business allows credit on different lines from those normally seen in trade credit.

The LME has clients in the metal and mining industry all over the world. They use the LME for lots of reasons, for example, to buy or sell forward for commercial purposes, for hedging, to lock in a price for their product for a year or two, i.e. a form of price insurance.

Credit refers to the amount by which the contract a client has made may be losing him money. The credit line is the extent to which Rudolf Wolff will not call on the client to top up that difference. The extent of this credit is determined by the credit committee. The credit committee which Francis chairs is made up of two other directors plus the credit manager and his assistant. The LME business is highly regulated and each month the members have to file returns to the regulatory body. Overexposure on credit might lead to a deficiency in financial resources, resulting in being disciplined or fined.

The amount of their valuation or 'open position' is monitored on a daily basis. If clients exceed their credit line they are immediately asked to pay the excess that day – not tomorrow or next week, but that day. Also, when the contract matures the money must be paid into the bank that day.

Credit people have to tread a difficult narrow path between being tough enough to collect the money and at the same time maintaining the good relationship with clients that account executives expect.

The credit committee, which meets once a month, brings Francis into formal contact with his credit manager. Credit lines are discussed in open forum. Each morning the credit manager reviews the previous day's business and discusses individual cases with the account executives (brokers). There is constant communication during the day between the credit people and the brokers. The brokers in their turn require up-to-the-minute credit and transaction information. This way the credit department is fully integrated into the mainstream company activity. In fact 'success through teamwork' is the theme of Francis's address in the Rudolf Wolff information brochure.

He sees the credit manager as very much a specialist. In the 27 years he has been with the company there have only been four credit managers

3.3 Interview 3

Steven Jacques of Evode Powder Coatings, the Midlands industrial paint manufacturer, a company in the Evode Group, has a strong customer care bias – he signs all the credit notes. Thus a vital link in the commercial chain between customer, company mistakes and the chief executive enables him to keep a realistic grasp on day-to-day operations. This is a clear message to the workforce that their performance is being monitored at the highest level.

Steven feels that credit and collections have become more of a competitive issue where his credit team are having to work harder and harder to get cash in (against a background of more professionalism in credit people, a recession and business in general trying to improve cashflow by paying later), and they have to be tactful in how they go about it. Yet, if they don't get it right the business suffers. It is vital to the company to get it right.

He sees that there are still some options open to him to make his credit and collections more competitive. This could involve improving the monitoring of customer service. He could do this by collecting selected customer feedback information, analysing it and responding more accurately to customers.

Though he feels that the level of communication in EPC between departments is good, he is always willing to look at ways of improving communications. Changing the management structure so that the credit department reports to the marketing/sales director might gain a more coordinated company approach in responding to customers. But any change like this would need to be carefully thought through. Such a change might be contemplated when a new computer system was being reviewed.

Steven receives a credit report at the end of each month, which includes a debtors aged listing. He looks more closely at the older debts and the customers who have exceeded their credit limits. He also asks his salesforce to keep a watchful eye on how customers are progressing. 'On the odd occasion when businesses have failed it has not shown up on any computer printout.'

Steven considers that credit people are specialists and

therefore he would prefer their specialist skills to stay within the credit department. His is a relatively small company with 150 employees and the opportunities for moving the credit manager to another job to broaden his experience do not arise at present. However, a recent merger with a sister company in the group may change things.

Steven says 'credit can be seen as merely getting cashflow right, but there are opportunities to use the function's experience throughout the company to integrate the company team spirit'.

3.4 Interview 4

David Blythe of Xpelair, the air conditioning manufacturing arm of GEC, looks at credit in terms of the capital employed being affected by the amount of unplanned credit allowed to or taken by his customers as directly affecting his company's ability to operate.

He recognizes that while Xpelair tries to collect debts quickly, his customers and suppliers are trying to do likewise. He tries to maintain a balance between recovery and payment of debt.

His credit management operation covers the range of services from credit vetting and billing through to cash collection. He makes a conscious effort to encourage the credit management team to have a good rapport with customers. All of this is achieved in an unstructured way and he wonders if it could be improved. For example, a more structured operation would capture a wealth of customer information which would be of value to them in managing the business. While this information is already received, it is not on a disciplined structured basis. David thinks that customer information is a resource that is under-utilized not only in his business but also probably in many others.

In terms of cash collection, he feels that it is important to know why the customers are not paying on time, and not just that the payments are late. If it is because they are dissatisfied with the product or service they are receiving, rather than that they are having cashflow problems, it is up to the credit department to find out quickly, and apply itself to solving the problem. 'The art is to deal with customers' queries as quickly and effectively as possible, since this eliminates an element which my company can do something about.'

Debit notes cause particular problems. The predicament arises from the way the product routes its way to the end comsumer. Customers are electrical wholesalers in the main, who supply electrical contractors and they in turn install the product in commercial or domestic premises. If the product is not satisfactory to the end consumer it is ultimately returned through the chain for a credit note. The problem is deciding at which point the product proved unsatisfactory.

Perhaps it was originally defective, or it became so at the contractor stage, or maybe it was used in a situation for which it was not intended. In order to learn and so prevent the situation happening again, Xpelair needs to find out exactly what happened.

In many cases, by the time the product is returned, it has been played with to such an extent that it is impossible to determine what the problem might have been. This affects not only future planning but also current deductions from payment cheques (by debit notes).

Even when the reason for an individual return of product is known, there may be a further more complicated step to take before the problem can be solved. If it happens that the contractor misuses the product and it is subsequently returned as faulty, the contractor's perception is that the product is faulty. The contractor may not be right, but it is the contractor's perception that has to be tackled.

David feels that 'far too often we are dealing with perceptions and not with reality. But we have nonetheless got to tackle the perceptions. We ignore perceptions at our peril.' He adds 'You may have all the statistics at your disposal to confirm that the products are reliable. So why is someone saying otherwise? The statistics have to be put aside to deal with the customer's complaint.'

He feels that when a query is answered quickly and effectively, far from that customer telling his friends what a rotten product it is, he will praise the service.

In order to look at these problems and to integrate the areas dealing with customers a small task force has been set up. Their objective is to come up with improvement suggestions. Members of the team include sales and service people and the credit manager.

David sees the credit manager as a specialist. This is perhaps because of the way Xpelair is structured. However, he believes that the broader the exposure of the individual manager to other aspects of the business, the better that manager will be in his discipline. He would like to move faster to achieve this kind of integrated management. He sees promotion possibilities for each of the disciplines as a way of encouraging ambitious managers, including the credit manager.

He believes that we in the United Kingdom carry too many specialists, that attitudes must change so that managers have broader skills and more general knowledge of business.

3.5 Interview 5

Tom Farmer of the Edinburgh-based Kwik-Fit Group initially closed down the credit accounts of an acquisition in 1980. However Kwik-Fit couldn't ignore the growth in the fleet car market and entered this market, a credit business, in 1987.

After two years of growth way beyond expectations, the internal computer systems and procedures came under stress from increasing customer queries and overdue debts. As Tom puts it 'we took our eye off the ball'. The course of action he took to correct this was both unusual and dramatic. He asked customers to pay all unqueried items and guaranteed that within a month they would either settle the query, if it was the fault of Kwik-Fit, or issue a credit note. This was a clear message to the workforce to treat customer queries urgently, as well as giving customers a service upon which they could rely.

Kwik-Fit in their turn deal with their suppliers in the same way. They will pay their bills on time and want credit notes for unsolved queries. If they are having any trouble with a supplier, they will call them in and sit around a table to solve queries before the month end.

The credit department is responsible for cash collection, cash allocation of cheques and obtaining answers to customers' queries from the service people. The authorization of credit notes is the responsibility of the service people. Since this directly impacts on their profitability it has the effect of improving performance.

For the fleet market sector of the business the credit account is held in the name of the car fleet customer. It is the car driver – often a salesperson or company executive – who is the direct contact with Kwik-Fit. He asks for service at a service centre. The service people assess what's to be done and ring the fleet office for an order number. Details of the work are fed into the system at the service centre and an invoice is raised overnight at HQ.

Each month the areas where service is not satisfactory are discussed and correcting instructions/advice are issued to the service centres. A point of sales information service is currently being further developed where the centre will have to include additional information required by the customer before the invoice can be input for invoicing. For example, if the customer requires mileage information, that must be included. This will help to reduce queries but also is commercially vital as it enables customers to monitor their fleets and become more cost effective.

Tom Farmer believes his credit operation is unique, and he bases this belief on the fast growth rate of his credit business. This is due to the availability of the service, the turnaround time of the work and the efficiency of his operation. He feels that primarily the credit manager is a specialist, but that he should know the business. Tom would want a new manager to spend the first four months in a service centre. He is in favour of moving people around the organization. The credit manager has, through experience, the ability to work in other areas.

Tom says 'a good credit manager is there to solve customer queries'.

He is totally committed to customer service and wants 'to go one stage further than aiming to have customers that are

100% satisfied'. He wants his 'customers to be delighted with our service'.

3.6 Interview 6

Mike Featherstone of Wade Furniture Makers, part of a Nottingham-based furniture group, says recession highlights the importance of credit management and cashflow. Although this has not been a problem for Wade – it is a family firm that has been trading since the 1880s without cashflow problems – it has recently tightened its monitoring of customers' payment habits. Relaxed payment trends can now be detected earlier, so allowing time to make low-key approaches.

Credit vetting, credit limits, cash collection and cash allocation are all centred in the same area. Order processing is a sales office function. The company is particularly helped by the industry's accepted standard payment terms which include discount inducements for weekly payments.

The group counts customer care as a main priority and this has superseded considerations of other functions. The furniture business is a friendly personal business. Therefore, it is easier than in most other business sectors to get to know the customers.

However, this is not left to chance. Customer information is regarded as vital. All customer complaints are logged and monitored, then analysed under 19 separate headings. These are reviewed once a month with particular interest focused on response solving time and quality of response. Where an item is returned faulty it is given back to the person who made it, for correction in the worker's own time.

The customers will not be asked to pay until the item is corrected and returned, even if the item being repaired is only a fraction of the total charge. The onus for hold-up is, therefore, placed at the door of the originator. This encourages the worker to get it right first time. It also sends a clear message to the customer that payment is only requested for goods that are absolutely top quality.

Mike takes 'outside' customer advice seriously. In the past 18 months two customer surveys have been done and improvements are being implemented in the areas highlighted as needing attention. Nothing stands still. The business is growing and stretching resources. Improvement programmes take time.

There was one improvement Mike was able to make very quickly. The survey showed that customers liked to speak to just one person in the company. So Mike divided the human resources into geographical areas. This further improved communications with customers.

Mike estimates that the monthly board meeting can spend from 25 to 50% of the time discussing customer issues. Included in this will be a paper from the sales director on what customers think about the company in any particular month, as well as the 19 customer complaints analysis reports. He reviews the monthly debtors aged listing.

How should credit people impress him? 'Do it nicely.'

3.7 Interview 7

David Willis of the Micrelec Group, a Surrey-based company offering systems and expertise to the petroleum industry, says 'credit management is the job of everyone in the company'.

There are four complementary companies in the group. Each one sells to the same customers in the main. Micrelec sells products two different ways:

(1) 70% of the business is conducted with major oil companies. Credit payment terms are included as an integral part of the marketing package.

(2) 30% of sales come through the efforts of the direct field salesforce who are paid commission.

David has recently introduced changes to make the group more competitive. Top of this list of changes is improvement in customer service. Not far behind this is the push to integrate further traditionally independent company functions. For example, the field salesforce is now responsible for:

- identifying the need;
- getting the order;
- making sure that the product is delivered;
- ensuring that the product is installed;
- positively confirming that the customer is satisfied with the product and service;
- cash collection.

This just about keeps the salesforce in touch with all aspects of the commercial process. A salesperson gets commission when the cash is received.

As a result of what David thinks is a medium-term cash collection problem in the industry, and to ensure cashflow stability, Micrelec has adopted discount inducements to customers who pay earlier than their payment terms require. David says 'credit terms are very much part of our marketing mix'.

Monitoring customer service is something he strives to do and it occupies his thoughts all the time. He remembers back to the time when he first started the company 'with my wife's housekeeping money. We always seemed to achieve the impossible and were paid in cash.' He believes he is ahead of his competitors, all blue chip companies, on the quality of product and service. Every 18 months he commissions an outside consultancy to carry out a customer survey checking the level of customer satisfaction.

As a way of keeping an everyday finger on the customer pulse Micrelec is now involved in a total quality improvement programme. The programme includes an input from the direct field salesforce's customers. When the product is delivered/ installed and before any payment is requested the salesperson asks the customer to complete a questionnaire confirming whether the product/service is satisfactory. A customer service manager has been appointed to analyse, act and report on comments. The customer service manager reports directly to the sales and marketing director. Where there has been a problem with the product or service the customer service people are responsible for collecting the debt.

David is considering a further management structure change in formally linking the credit controller with customer service. This might improve both the integration of customer contact functions and also the career progression for credit people.

He feels that with four accountants on the board of six directors to worry about profitability and balance sheet items this gives him the time to concentrate on the operational ability of the group. He concentrates on (i) making sure that all his customers are satisfied and (ii) having the cash in the bank to be able to keep the service operating.

3.8 Interview 8

Gordon Green of JCB Credit sees his company's role as extending credit to customers of the JCB Group.

JCB Credit was formed by a joint venture with the National Westminster Bank Group. NatWest took 74% of the shares and JCB 26%. In 1969 Gordon was approached to develop the credit business potential. JCB did not go into the venture to take profits from JCB Credit. However, Gordon says 'The availability of extended credit facitities has enabled the Group to win orders and increase JCB's market penetration'.

JCB sells all its UK products through six JCB franchise dealers. JCB sells to these dealers on a cash-with-order basis. So nothing goes down the manufacturing line that isn't paid for already. However, the board calculated that by extending credit to the dealers' customers JCB would both offer a better service to these customers and increase sales.

- Funding comes through the NatWest treasury desk or Gordon can take 'year money' (finances which are available at a fixed rate of interest, bought now and fixed for a year). For instance, in August 1990 he borrowed at a rate which was above the then going rate, anticipating that interest rates would rise. The rates subsequently rose steeply in the following months. His forward buying of finance increased his profit margins.

Does he feel comfortable sitting between manufacturer and banker? Which does he lean towards? Gordon, as an ex-Royal

Marine, points out that Royal Marines learn at an early stage that they are neither soldier nor sailor but a bit of both. This was good training for his present job. His salary is paid by NatWest and his office is across the road from the main JCB complex in Rocester, Staffordshire. He was taken on to develop a JCB idea and this gave him the chance to use his experience and innovative skills. Sometimes he wears a NatWest hat and sometimes a JCB one. Perhaps his car registration number gives him away: JCB 52!

He is very much aware of how the economic climate affects the cashflow of customers and he keeps in mind a JCB philosophy, promoted by the Group Chief Executive Gilbert Johnston, of 'generating customer warmth'.

He 'lends to *people* and not balance sheets'. He considers whether the people have the ability to sustain their business for the duration of the loan rather than concentrate on financial ratios using out-of-date financial accounts information. 'Predicting customers' sustainability over the period of the loan cannot be learnt from 18-month-old financial data.' Gordon says 'If had to look at classic balance sheet ratios in determining who we lent to in the construction industry we would not lend to anybody'.

He constantly strives to offer his customers a better service than that offered by his competitors, for example:

- JCB Credit wrote to all its major customers early in 1990, predicting the worst recession for 30 years in the building and construction industry. The company offered to reschedule their repayments over a longer period with a view to halving their monthly payments. This went down very well, as it enabled and is still enabling companies to spread further a very scarce asset – cash.

- He then reviewed the cash strains of JCB's six dealers who were suffering in the recession from having to pay cash with order. Gordon came up with another well-received scheme for the dealers.

    Under the scheme, the dealers would pay 25% of the wholesale product price, and 100% of the VAT charge immediately, while JCB Credit would pay the 75% balance. JCB

Credit would then allow the dealers 90 days' free credit. JCB Sales would pay JCB Credit the interest. At the end of 90 days the dealers would pay the interest. This would give the dealer a big incentive to sell the product fast.

- JCB customers began to ask for finance for other products too. This the company agreed to do providing that the products were not manufactured by competitors of JCB.

These services have enhanced the image of JCB. They have also bonded customers to JCB for the longer term.

Gordon is conscious of the need to maintain good quality customer service. Having been a pioneer in offering this particular type of company extended credit, he wants to ensure that they stay in front. He explains 'We will sell the service that is better for the customers but not always best for JCB Credit'. Gilbert Johnston describes JCB Credit as 'the lubrication that gets the product from the factory into the customers' hands in the shortest timeframe possible. JCB's aim is to look long term and keep their competitive edge sustainable.'

Gordon says that within his own company employees consider a recipient of their work as a customer. For example, his administration people look on the field salespeople as their customers as much as external purchasers of JCB equipment.

Monitoring JCB Credit contact with customers is a constant process. When his people call on customers they must first write down on their daily call sheet what they expect to achieve before they go into the meeting, and then what actually happened and the outcome. Gordon personally reviews these sheets.

He believes 'that people buy people' before they buy the product. He uses two outside sources for training staff and the training is directed towards giving a better customer service.

He has replicated the JCB Credit methods in JCB's overseas operations, taking on local partners who understand the local conditions and market. They are, therefore, well placed to cater for the open European market in 1992.

Gordon Green considers himself to be the chief executive of a credit sales organization, unique in the way it does things and hoping to stay that way.

3.9 Interview 9

Sue Tramontini of Tramontini & Partners, says 'in a small company like ours cashflow is absolutely vital to us'.

T&P is a programme production company specializing in corporate television programmes for business, government and education. The company has a small but loyal customer base and runs four to five major contracts a year. Client satisfaction plays a key role in maintaining and developing the company with two-thirds of turnover being repeat business.

Getting paid is fortunately not a problem, since there is a recognized payment method which is largely acknowledged by clients. The pattern is:

- an invoice covering one-third of the final contract charge is presented to the client for payment on the signing of the contract;
- a second invoice equal to one-third of the contract charge is presented on completion of the principal photography, i.e. the main shooting;
- the final invoice is presented on delivery of the first finished copy.

In Sue's business clients may want the opportunity to make last minute changes and sometimes hold back 10% of the contract charge.

The terms of payment are discussed and agreed before any work starts. Sue would expect to be paid immediately the invoices are presented and would get directly involved herself if the debt became more than 30 days old.

T&P's contract is based on the standard industry contract which Sue was involved in drawing up in her role as Chairman of the International Visual Communication Association. Companies who commission a lot of work, and government departments, draw up their own contract but these are very similar to the industry standard.

All communication with clients is recorded methodically and notes are made in the clients' files. The business is prone to change of mind/lapse of memory about what was said/agreed subsequent to the contact being signed. Therefore, Sue feels that keeping notes on everything that happens is crucial to retain straightforward dealings with clients. In fact she feels she has made a success of this when clients ring her because they know that her notes are more accurate then their own!

Normally the producer controls all contract with the client including any queries and cash collection. There was a time when some large companies took advantage of their size to squeeze longer payment periods out of small companies. Sue feels that this attitude is now more the exception than the rule because of CBI and government initiatives to help small firms.

In fact she has found that some large organizations now have a policy of giving priority to the invoices of small companies. But before starting a contract Sue still believes in talking to her clients about their attitude to paying small businesses.

3.10 Interview 10

Paul Hodgkinson, Chairman of the Lincoln-based Simons Group, says 'good quality credit management is fundamental to the success of any company'.

About 85% of Simons' work is with regular business partners and clients. These clients are mainly 'blue chip' and require quality work and fast delivery. The work includes a lot of what Paul regards as fast track fitting out projects which require management-intensive skills, together with craft skills. The company completes many traditional work projects too.

At any one time Simons is running approximately 1000 live projects, 2000 completed but not yet finalized and 2000 in the process of being put together. Examples of the kinds of project recently completed are 'the most advanced food factory in the world at Grimsby, the most advanced ballbearing factory in the world for a Japanese client and two restaurants in Moscow'.

Paul regards his credit management team as one of the finest in the construction industry. He does not employ a credit manager as such. Everyone in the company is involved in credit management. The responsibility is given to the person managing the project or group of projects. In turn they are monitored by a team of accountants. Managing directors monitor the whole process in their respective divisional companies.

There are two groups of people in the financial management team: accountants and surveyors. He considers surveyors as number crunching administrators or 'building accountants'. Surveyors manage the individual projects. When payments are missed by clients the accountants will bring this to the attention of the surveyors. Sales and marketing people are often called in to unlock overdue debts because of their close relationships with clients.

The financial management team produces day-to-day information on creditors and debtors. At any time they have a series of quite complex cost/value reconciliations which are actually being carried out on projects on a monthly basis. Paul feels that it would not be possible for one person (for example a credit manager) to manage the group's debts.

Simons concentrates a lot of time getting things right at the front end. The group will try to deal with regular business partners to build up a good working relationship. Managers will pay close attention at the negotiation stage and complete credit checks. They will take into account the quality of the work of business partners and subcontractors, the payment record of the client, and when they go to the open market for work (where the usual criterion for successful tendering is supplying the lowest tender price) they will take into account how this side of the market operates payment terms – pay when paid. Generally, Paul expects to get paid within the negotiated payment terms on the strength of the quality of the group's work and its record for delivering within tight time scales.

3.11 Summary

- All the views presented in the interviews speak for themselves and I am very grateful to the chief executives and chairmen for making their valuable time available.

PART II

Immediate Improvement in Cashflow and Profitability through Credit Management

OVERVIEW

The credit department is a fairly specialized function in most people's eyes. So the tendency for credit managers to shunt staff off into this and that specialized corner within the department is puzzling. The normal areas of specialization within the credit department are: credit vetting, 'legal', cashiering/accounts reconciliation, cash collection, customer queries and high value/low value customer accounts.

The philosophy of getting everyone involved in everything is much more rewarding. This makes life more interesting for the individuals. They see more of the business and can more readily appreciate the trials of others in different departments of the company. Other benefits include easier holiday cover and training of potential credit managers.

It is possible for the credit department to monitor the quality of operations in all functions of the company. This can be accomplished very simply by passing on the day-to-day customer information the department receives to the other company departments. This encourages better understanding of the issues and maintains standards.

The issues are not always clear. There are sometimes fine distinctions between what is the more acceptable approach to customers. For example, the attitude of relieving them of the burden of holding money for you may be a softer approach than extracting cash from them.

In each customer call the quality of the conversation, the professionalism of the message and attitude to the customer's people, will count towards the next time. You may not want to give them the impression that they have done something wrong when they have missed your pay-by date. It is far better to indicate that you are at fault for not getting round to having a chat with them earlier. Attention to detail is all-important.

Maintaining standards is primarily about looking after the customers and making sure the workforce is happy doing so. A happy workforce is one that is well trained and motivated.

Part II reveals the sort of detail that encourages a review of the constituents of the credit department. It also includes a complete and very practical operational guide on how to run a modern credit department.

Definition of credit management

Credit management can embrace:

(1) Credit vetting
(2) Order processing
(3) Billing
(4) Accounts receivable
(5) Cash collection
(6) Query control/customer feedback information.

CREDIT VETTING

Company reports: annual financial accounts from the customer, Companies House or credit status agencies.
Trade references: two trade references from customer's suppliers.
Bank reference: this will virtually only confirm that the customer has a bank account.
Credit application form: this will confirm practical details of the customer's business.
Credit limits: flexible and manageable.

ORDER PROCESSING

On-line or manual: fast friendly and positive response is crucial.
Accuracy: get it right the first time.

Credit trips: alert the credit department that a customer requires credit in excess of his current credit limit.
Order date versus delivery date versus invoice date: ideally all three dates should be the same.

BILLING

Invoice/statement design: each has a message for customers. Is this message clear?
Accuracy of information: all details *must* be correct. It helps if the details are always input only once.
Speed of procedure: an invoice that is received quickly by a customer enables that customer to include the debt in their cash flow at an early date.
Volume: volume spread evenly through the month enables everyone including the customer to plan their workloads.

ACCOUNTS RECEIVABLE

Cashiering: a routine for fast banking of money received saves bank overdraft charges.
Reconciliation of accounts: clean customer statements are easier to pay. Accurate cash allocation depends on attention to detail.
Speed: customers are owed a speedy service when they pay. Same-day receipt of cash and account allocation of the cash should be an acknowledged target.

CASH COLLECTION

Credit period: the credit period which is expressed in days is the basic accepted measurement of the cash collection performance.
Cash collection cycle: cash collection should start at the earliest time. Waiting until the customer's account is overdue for payment is asking for trouble.
Cash collection techniques: experience shows that close attention to certain detail gets better results. Asking questions is far superior to demanding answers.
Customer performance records: the better and more accurate the

information on the customer, the greater the success. It will show up in conversations. Such attention to detail is not lost on the customers.

Internal co-ordination: in some companies communication and understanding inside the organization are not up to the standard of the communication with customers. This is always exposed to customers.

Competition: includes not only the people in the same industry but also all other suppliers of products and services to customers.

QUERY CONTROL / CUSTOMER FEEDBACK INFORMATION

Value £: experience shows that unless queries are closely monitored outstanding queries will average 12% of company turnover.

Volume of queries: volume will point to the number of dissatisfied customers.

Response times: customer queries enable the company to show how effective it is at caring for customers.

Results: monitoring performance will produce better results.

Marketing feedback: the value of the information that can be given by customers is far superior to the information of market research companies.

A SUMMARY OF THE CREDIT MANAGEMENT POSITION

- More than cash collection.
- More than allocation of cash.
- More than answering customers' queries.

Tom Peters in *In Search of Excellence* says that 'Most successful companies get their best ideas from customers'.

Collecting information is as much a part of credit management as collecting money. It could be the next launch pad for corporate success.

How to Get Started

4.1 Credit vetting

Risks vary tremendously. There is a need to get to grips with the sort of risks being taken, and what these risks mean in terms of the business. Generally, the highest profits are accompanied by the highest risks.

Traditional high-risk industries like fashion clothes, restaurants and music, where you win some and lose some, make profits on winning more than losing. This is in contrast to industries like the food business where the margins are low and the risks not so pronounced. Good credit vetting can contribute to profits by reducing the risks. The key to making the right decision depends on the amount and accuracy of the information you hold.

It is not always possible to get all the information you would like before making a decision. So special allowances have to be made in the profits forecasts for an acceptable level of mistakes. There is, however, no reason to get careless.

There are different levels of information. Industrial information can give pointers where local or individual customer information is unavailable. You could broadly accept orders from *The Times* top 100 companies without too much checking. Though a check on their paying record might be advised.

GETTING THE INFORMATION

Company reports

The potential customer can supply a copy of its annual report. This will show how the company wants to be presented to the world of shareholders. Since companies want to keep their shareholders on the basis of both their track record and, more importantly, what they can achieve, the report concentrates on the future which should suit credit people. By the time the credit people get the report the company should have achieved some of its forecasts.

The more you read the more you can read between the lines. Most company reports are not too exciting. You could be forgiven for thinking that they were all written by the same person. When they say they are looking forward to the next year, this may be because the previous one was disastrous. If they refer to a tough year ahead, there's going to be a fall in profits.

Company reports are also available from other sources. Credit status agencies supply reports in various forms: on-line; set of three-year annual accounts, sometimes with comments; and in shortened versions just giving one or two details in directory book format. Before approaching an agency it is a good idea to work out what you want from it, even if it eventually changes your mind. Spare the time to contact all of them. The principle being that it is better spending the time getting the correct system at the start of the credit management work cycle than having to rely on the 'Help Industry' at the end. A list of agencies appears in Figure 4.1.

The following is a list of some of the status enquiry agencies and financial information service companies. For further information contact the Institute of Credit Management on 0780 56777.

Infolink 081–686–7777
- instant information – 1 million files
- customer enquiry system – set-up price £150.00
- reportage service
- report cost from £1.00 for basics to £17.50 for detailed analysis

Infocheck 071–377–5615
- claims to be the most detailed and comprehensive database in the UK
- access through Telecom Gold, Pergamon, Prestel, Istel, Kompass and Mercury Link 7500
- basic information on 1.2 million companies and full reports on 180,000 public and private companies. Some 3,000 companies are added to the list each week.
- the basic information is free to subscribers – full reports 75 ratios £4–£9
- works out at £12.50 for host system reports

Figure 4.1 Enquiry agencies and financial information services.

ICC   071–250–3922
- Viewdata service, most frequently used
- three-tier detailed information 100,000 companies listed
- basic information on 2 million companies
- a number of host systems take Viewdata – Dialog, Data Star, Datastream, Guardian Business Information
- pay as you go – basic £1.00; complete report £5–£7

Jordans   071–253–3030
- five-tier database – 2 million companies
- files incorporated into Kompass on-line services
- access through Telecom Gold, Istel or Pergamon
- £72.00 per hour (and up to £6.00 for fuller information)
- volume discounts available – no subscription charge

Dunn and Bradstreet   071–377–4350
- total UK records 1.3 million – international 15 million companies
- pay up-front – £20.00 normal report, pretty comprehensive
- other products – who owns whom 25,000 parent companies
- Key British Enterprises 20,000 companies
- Dunn's Market Identifiers 200,000 companies
- prices £70–£125 per hour

Kompass   0342–26972
- covers 115,000 companies – can go through Dialog
- no joining fee – pay as you go
- charge per hour £30–£70 depending on type of search
- have to pay at least £70.00 in advance
- small fee for training

Finsbury Data   071–250–1122
- background information from 1980 extracts from 1000 newspapers and magazines
- three services – Textline, Newsline, Dataline

McCarthy   0985–215151
- joint venture with FT and Datasolve (Thorn EMI)
- offers up-to-date newspaper information on leading companies
- registration fee is £100.00
- standard connect fee is £84.00 per hour – substantial discounts for regular users

Figure 4.1 *Contd.*

Credit application form and referee letters (see Figures 4.2–4.6)

These should be designed to give practical details of the potential customer and the minimum information you require to be able to dispatch the first order. As it is the first official bit of paper from your company to theirs it will set the tone for your future business relationship. The customer's name, for instance, needs to be spelt correctly.

```
Dear

APPLICATION FOR A CREDIT ACCOUNT

We take pleasure in enclosing a credit application form
following your request for credit account facilities
with us.

Our terms of payment are as follows:

     'Please pay within 30 days of the invoice date.'

Our response will depend to a great extent upon the form
being returned fully completed and the time your referees
take to reply to our enquiries.

Please mail this form direct to the above address for the
attention of the undersigned.

Yours sincerely




CREDIT DEPARTMENT
```

Figure 4.2 Application for a credit account.

When the credit application form is returned it should be the most accurate document on the customer details you receive. So it is worth reviewing it carefully. Specimens are given in Figures 4.2 to 4.4. The form includes a request to name three referees: one bank and two trade. However, in the absence of these referees, say in the case of a new start-up company or sole proprietor without any trading experience, you would take up character references. These might come from a past employer or, in the case of someone who has just finished school, a school teacher.

If the form is completed in a sloppy way – i.e. some questions are not answered, handwriting looks like a doctor's prescription, there may be a coffee stain or worse, it is signed by the office cat – it is necessary to draw certain conclusions. Is this the kind of business that would be good for your company? If these people treat you like this how do they treat their customers? And what implication has that for your company? I have in my time as a credit manager made decisions solely based on how the credit application was completed. Some people take exception to form filling. Take this example.

It is not only the fly-by-night companies you have to look out for in the record industry. As in any industry there are the customers with clout who keep you hanging on.

However, these companies are the sum total of the individuals who work there. Clout can always be diluted, isolated and made to see reason.

I remember receiving a returned application form from the company secretary of a newly formed company. Two large companies had joined forces to run the venture. He had omitted the names of the company directors. I rang him to confirm the names.

He took the request badly. He was terribly offended that I did not take his word and that of the named companies. I pointed out to him that without knowing the names of the people who ran his company we could be dealing with anyone.

He was getting more irritated by the minute. I could feel him thinking 'just who is this annoying little parasite?' It was as if I'd asked him for his wife's phone number. It then struck me that maybe he did not know the directors' names. In the end I got the names from Companies House.

The implication that I drew here was that the culture of the company, if the company secretary's attitude was anything to go by, was going to be offhand with its customers.

Years later I did deal with them as a customer. I have to say that the association did not last long. The unfortunate thing is that although I still like the product I couldn't stand the service.

The questions to ask yourself when asking for information are as follows:

- Is it a reasonable question?
- Would I give out such information?
- Is it necessary and relevant?
- Will they find it easy to answer?

CREDIT ACCOUNT APPLICATION FORM
1. Name and address of Paying Office

_____

_____

Telephone No ....
2. Goods Delivery/Services: Name and address

_____

_____

Telephone No ....
3. Name and address for Invoices, Credit Notes, Statements and future
correspondence to be mailed to (if different from above, if not invoices and
statements will be mailed to Paying Office).

_____

_____

4.1. The concern is constituted as (please delete those not applicable)
    (a) A sole proprietorship
    (b) A partnership
    (c) A company with unlimited liability
    (d) A private/public company registered in the UK/overseas with limited
         liability
4.2.   (a) Date accounts last filed ....
    (b) Enclose copy of latest Profit/Loss and Balance Sheet
5. The date and details of formation, affiliations or connections with other
concerns are as follows: please use other side of page.

Figure 4.3 Credit account application form.

The questions need regular reviewing. Complacency can set in. Language changes. Letters to the paper used to finish 'Your humble servant': not any more. Now it is more likely to be 'Annoyed from Staines' or 'Disgusted from Hampstead'.

The same set of questions may be asked of hundreds of potential customers each month, but these customers only get the form once. They may take exception to it. It is wise to try to accommodate their perceptions of what information is reasonable for them to give as against the information required. After all the marketing department tried hard to include customers' perceptions in their marketing strategy. It would be a pity to dent the image at such a crucial stage. Undoing their work can lose

6. The Principals of the concern and Directors, if any:
_____

_____

7. The name and address of our bankers is:
_____

_____

8. You may apply to the two following concerns for trade references

Name	Name
Address	Address
Account No.	Account No.

9.1. Our estimated value of goods to be purchased from you each month is
£.................
9.2. Our opening order value is £...............
The above information is given in confidence and to my knowledge is accurate in all respects.

Signature _____ Date_____

Full name of signatory in block capitals
_____

Position in concern
_____

Figure 4.3 *Contd.*

customers. Without customers there would be no call for a credit manager. Some companies do ask for unnecessary information. Complacency is never healthy.

Asking easy-to-answer questions should get fast replies. Asking the right questions should get more accurate replies. The faster and more accurate the replies the more debt you can take on. Taking on the highest possible debt level enables sales to grow and the credit manager to become almost indispensable. This is something to bear in mind.

Sad to say there was one unfortunate exception that I had to let slip through the net while working in the record industry.

Dear

We have been asked to open a CREDIT ACCOUNT for the above
named. They have passed us your name to act as a
reference. They require goods to the value of £.........
each month.

Your guidance in advising us, by answering the questions
set out below, would be much appreciated. A stamped
addressed envelope is enclosed.

We thank you in anticipation for your information which
will be treated in strict confidence. We would be happy
to offer you a similar service should the need arise.

Yours sincerely

CREDIT DEPARTMENT

Is the account settled to your payment terms?   ....

If not, approximately how late do they pay?   ....

What is the normal credit allowed?   £..........

How long have you known them?   ....

Is caution advised?   ....

Figure 4.4 Trade reference letter.

I got a call from the doting parents of a young man who was very
keen to open a record shop.

He himself could not legally take on debts which he would
need in order to stock the shop with records and tapes. They were
retired and they owned their own house. They did not have a
mortgage. They were prepared to mortgage their property in
order to raise the finance for their son's intended venture. They

```
PRIVATE AND CONFIDENTIAL


Dear Sirs

Re:

Your name has been given to us by the above who wish to
open a credit account with us on normal monthly terms.

We would appreciate confirmation by you that an account of
£......... outstanding at any one time would be considered
a reasonable trade risk.

We enclose a stamped addressed envelope for your reply to
our bankers:




Thank you for your assistance which we will treat in
strict confidence.


Yours sincerely



CREDIT DEPARTMENT


Encl: 1
```

Figure 4.5 Bank reference letter.

wanted advice on what to do and how to go about it.

Their son had no experience of working in a record shop. In fact he had never worked in any kind of business. Not a paper round (which I was prepared to consider) had come his way.

I tried to see 12 months ahead. All I could see were bailiffs. I had to advise caution.

However, I did not completely put them off. Perhaps he

Dear

We are delighted to be able to offer you credit facilities with our company. We have allocated you Account Number ....

We have attached, for your information, a copy of our letter to your buyer .... with an explanation of how to order product. To assist you further in understanding our way of doing things here, we set out below the way we will action your request for our products.

Most ordering is usually done on the telephone. Orders are dispatched on the day of order or the next day. All paperwork is dated on the day of dispatch (including picking note, delivery note and the invoice). You will receive an invoice a few days later. Statements are dated on the last working day each month. They include all entries of charges and payments up to and including that date. Statements are dispatched a few days later.

Any query should in the first instance be directed to the Credit Department. The person who will look after your account is ....

Our terms of payment are as follows:

    'Please pay within 30 days of the invoice date.'

We would like to take this opportunity to thank you for your custom and we look forward to a happy continuous business relationship.

Yours sincerely

CREDIT MANAGER

Figure 4.6 Letter offering credit facilities.

could gain experience by working in a record shop, or failing this in any shop. He needed to see and respond to customers. What about a stint at night school on a small business course? And before they mortgage their property either see their bank manager or come back and talk to me.

As I did not hear from them after this, I feel that they probably had a rethink.

Other sources of information

Several companies publish industrial comparison reports. They should mention where they get the information. The industrial reports normally include a set of business performance ratios by industry sector. These can be compared with the potential customer's business ratios. Because of the complexity of modern business it is not always easy to compare like with like.

For example, ICI we all know is a chemical company and so is BP Chemicals but who, hand on heart, could justify a comparison of financial ratios? Even if companies are manufacturing the same product they may be in different markets. It would not be wise to compare the DSO of a company solely engaged in exports with that of one just selling in the UK. The ratios do have their use. That use is limited. Recognizing this, it is, of course, useful to look at any kinds of comparison.

It is important to maintain industry contacts if only to be able to share in the complaints. Other credit people can help.

There are the media. It is really surprising what they can come up with. Accepting the saying 'you can't always believe what you read in the papers', there is no harm at all in talking to the people who write the news. Remember Watergate.

ANALYSIS OF INFORMATION

The analysis is all-important. Unfortunately much analysis is done after the event. This is because it is easier. It is not right but it is easy.

There is a whole industry involved in analysing failure. Somebody once said that the difference between doing the right thing as against doing what is right, is like rearranging the deckchairs on the *Titanic* rather than getting to grips with the imminent direction of the ship.

A company report is a snapshot of the accounts on one day. They are prepared to present the best possible picture. Converting the information to ratios allows a more compatible comparison of performance. It adds a further dimension to the analysis.

Business performance ratios

The industry ratios will be average ratios. They indicate the performance of the market as a whole. But it is important to keep in mind two provisos, especially if the potential customer is going to impact substantially on company sales:

- Be wise to the fact of what is being compared. Since it is highly unlikely that the comparison is exactly like with like, allowances for a margin of difference would be advisable. The way to do this is to keep in mind a balance between what is exact and what is a rough guide. This judgement is only gained by experience.

- Since the ratios are drawn from average figures there will be some companies that will be better than the average and some that will be worse. Comparing a company against the industry sector average is no substitute for getting the exact account figures of competitors to work out efficiency ratios.

Figure 4.7 comprises a set of figures which were extracted from the profit and loss account and balance sheet of a company in the office equipment manufacturers industry sector along with the average figures. The average figures are from ICC Publications Limited (see Figure 4.8). The company figures are converted to ratios so that a comparison can be made. The company is The Great Office Machine Company Limited or GOMC Limited for short. Each ratio is explained.

From the credit management point of view the questions are the following:

(1) Are they solvent?

(2) Do they pay their debts within our terms of payment?

A more long-term question about continued success ought to be included, just to keep the long-term view in perspective. Though this, to be accurate, is more a sales and marketing consideration.

The following figures were taken from the accounts of The Great Office Machine Company Limited for the years 1985/86 and 1984/85. This is followed by an extract from the pages of ICC's Industrial Performance Analysis.

		1985/86 (£'000s)		1984/85 (£'000s)	
Sales		366,695		343,113	
UK	36,298		36,032		
Operating profit		13,540	3.7%	13,568	4.5%
Net profit		8,245	2.2%	6,869	1.2%
Stocks		88,251	4.2 times*	84,716	4.1 times
Trade debtors		91,046	91 days	86,561	92 days
Cash		21,952		7,226	
Investments		959		19,223	
Total current assets		216,567		211,434	
Trade creditors		21,629	22 days	20,641	22 days
Other current creditors		71,843		64,182	
Total current liabilities		97,688		105,564	
Creditors long term		2,049		1,717	
Loans and overdrafts long term		41,580		33,100	

* Stock turnover = Sales over stocks

Comparison with the industry sector figures ICC Report

		GOMC Limited	Industry average
Pre-tax profit margin	%	2.2	11.2
Stock turnover	times per year	4.2	4.2
Liquidity		2.2	1.6
Quick ratio		1.3	1.0
Credit period (DSO)	days	91	67
Creditors' ratio	days	22	27

Figure 4.7 Figures from a company of office equipment manufacturers and averages from ICC.

ICC uses two ratios to test solvency.

(1) The liquidity ratio = current assets including quoted investments, expressed as a ratio of current liabilities. So to take the example of the 1985/86 year of office equipment manufacturers, the calculation would be as follows:

$$\frac{\text{Total current assets}}{\text{Total current liabilities}} \quad \frac{£473,285,000}{£237,785,000} = 2.0$$

(2) Quick ratio = the sum of debtors and other current assets *less* stocks divided by total current liabilities. This ratio

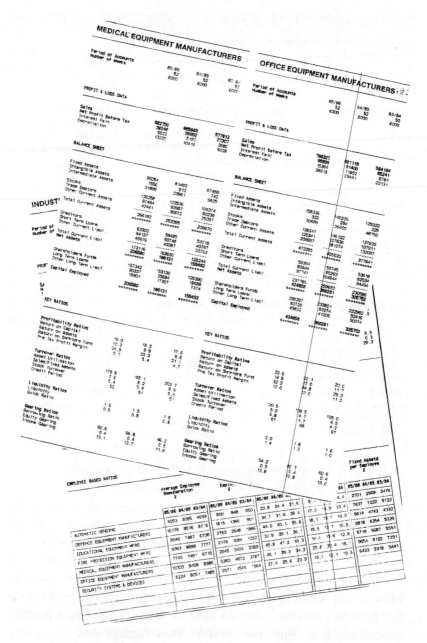

Figure 4.8 Comparison of figures from manufacturers.

Source: *Industrial Performance Analysis*, published by ICC Publications.

ignores stocks. It is, therefore, looking at the worth of the assets of a company in terms of the assets that can immediately be turned into cash. In some industries the stocks can be written down considerably, e.g. fresh food. In others it would take an expert to assess their value, e.g. aircraft spare parts. The calculation would be as follows:

$$\frac{\text{Total current assets } less \text{ stocks}}{\text{Total current liabilities}} \quad \frac{£335,038,000}{£237,785,000} = 1.4$$

Anything over 1.0 could be safely considered solvent. Therefore, GOMC Limited could be considered solvent.

However, it would not be prudent to apply this rule of thumb to every situation. In the cash and carry industry the quick ratio average for the industry works out at 0.3 and they survive happily. Nothing is ever clear-cut. The experience needed to distinguish between what is and is not reasonably acceptable is only gained by continual monitoring.

The creditors' ratio is normally used to work out how long a company takes to pay its customers. The formula is trade creditors divided by sales × 365. So to work out how long GOFMC Limited takes to pay its customers' accounts the calculation is as follows:

$$\frac{\text{Trade creditors}}{\text{Sales}} \quad \frac{£21,629,000}{£366,695,000} = \times 365 = 22 \text{ days}$$

This paying record would certainly come within most terms of payment. So the fact that the company appears solvent and pays its customers within terms of payment makes it an unusually good bet for a trouble-free business relationship. Therefore, it should be safe to offer credit.

However, although ratios are easy and concise measuring tools, they can also be traps. There is nothing wrong with the above calculation. But few of the other figures add up to the company's being super-efficient. So it is worth while investing a little more time to tease out a more accurate picture.

A more realistic view of when the company pays, may be to look at its credit period since it is probably a good bet that the company will collect its money first and then pay out its customers. This puts a different complexion on interpreting the length of time for the company to pay its accounts.

To calculate the credit period or DSO the formula is trade debtors over sales $\times$ 365:

$$\frac{\text{Trade debtors}}{\text{Sales}} \quad \frac{£91,046,000}{£366,695,000} \times 365 = 91 \text{ days}$$

This does not compare very well with the rest of the industry. The average DSO in the industry is 68 days. This means that GOMC Limited collects its money 23 days behind the average in the industry and, therefore, probably over a month after the leaders in the cash collection stakes.

There is yet a further aspect to consider. GOMC's DSO figures include a large element of export trade while the rest of the industry is mainly import or UK trade. Overseas terms of payment are generally spread over longer periods.

In some countries foreign currency and internal strife can cause payment difficulties. Even so if one customer whose business was in Beirut managed to pay according to payment terms throughout the 1970s why can't the rest make similar efforts? The only difference between him and other overseas customers was that he visited the factory and met the workforce.

The reason for the extension of credit to overseas customers is due to a poor understanding of their customs and culture. With more understanding of their needs, the reason for extending them longer credit periods would be invalidated.

Another pointer to managing GOMC's resources is its levels of profitability. Net profit before tax at 2.2% is about one-fifth of the average in the industry. Operating profit is deteriorating. Unless there is some extraordinary item in the accounts to explain these low figures it would have to be accepted as poor management of the company.

There is a large cash figure. In the light of the figures encountered so far this needs some explaining. It would be unusual for a company to hold such an amount at the bank. In this case there is fortunately an easy explanation. However, the explanation is only an assumption. There is in the industry an element of sales to customers who are financed by finance leasing companies. The cash at the bank is the payment by the leasing companies, presumably received in the current month.

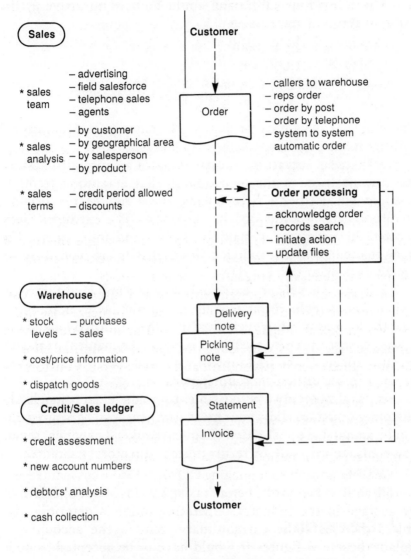

Figure 4.9 Order processing cycle.

Nonetheless it is still a large amount of cash seemingly sitting there doing nothing.

This adds to the true average payment period of GOMC Limited. Since, if it in effect has a significant element of cash sales, a point not taken into account in calculating the DSO, this should be put right in order to get at the true length of time taken to collect trade debts.

The following calculation could be used to arrive at the value in terms of days' sales.

91 days = £91,046,000
1 day = £ 1,000,505
cash   £21,952,000 = $\dfrac{£21,952,000}{£1,000,505}$ = 22 days

Therefore, 22 days plus 91 days = 113 days. GOGMC Limited collects its average trade debt in 113 days.

All these observations and calculations are intended to show the true position of the company so that extending credit to it could be justified. In reviewing these figures the original creditors' ratio should not be forgotten. The creditors' ratio showed that creditors are paid in 22 days. Perhaps they are. The trade references might indicate whether they are paid closer to the 22 days or to the 113 days.

The profit levels are extremely low and any creditor might feel uncomfortable about sustainable profit being maintained over the long term. However, even if GOMC Limited looked like it was perhaps too risky a venture for some companies to take on, credit managers have undoubtedly allowed credit to businesses in much more difficult circumstances.

It is almost always possible to trade even though the customer's business fails your most stringent test. Measures that can be adopted are post-dated cheques, bankers' cheques, seven-day credit terms, sale or return terms, directors' guarantee, or cash terms.

4.2 Decisions

Credit decisions are made all day every day. Each company lays down guidelines based on past experience, the current state of the market and what might happen in the future.

These decisions carry a certain amount of risk. The balancing of this risk is important. It should be balanced on the knowledge of the market and in particular of the customer requesting credit. Unless company guidelines are finely tuned into the marketplace they get caught up in other internal company procedures, not sympathetic with the credit department's views. These procedures seem destined to take the decision making away from the customer-orientated area and into a financial straitjacket.

Obviously this is not the same as advocating the abandonment of financial constraints. The consideration should tend towards thinking about what customers want, what they can afford and what part the credit department can play in supplying their needs.

The credit department that closely follows the marketing and sales philosophy stands a better chance of seeing past the sales hype – its own company's and that of the potential customer. It can add to the market information at the crucial time of first contact with the customer. This is because its routine, i.e. up front, allows it the time to look in the right place.

A customer-orientated credit department tends to look at the operational side of a customer's business. This is what makes the customer's business tick from day to day. It will get into this operational side more and more as it gets to know the customer better. An effective credit department gets to know the customers better than the customers know themselves. The reason for this is simple. In order to collect cash effectively the credit department must get to know all the procedures of the customer's company departments.

4.3 Summary

- Marketing decisions are often made on the basis of speculation and assumed knowledge of the marketplace. Few facts are involved. Credit decisions have more of a fact content but also include some dubious assumptions. If credit managers always felt comfortable about their decisions, their companies would not be doing much business. It is not that kind of a job. It is more of a hot seat.

Order Processing

Order processing starts at the switchboard. Switchboards vary tremendously. If the switchboard does not answer within the first three rings it can be considered slow. This reflects on your company.

There are some companies that answer on the first ring. This shows a willingness to save callers' time. There is only one company that I know of that manages to get the extension also to answer on the first ring. It is very impressive. It is IBM.

The companies that answer on the first ring and then keep you hanging on not only waste your time but run up your phone bill. So to get the first part right is not enough.

Order processing people must perform all the time. Customers must be made welcome every minute of every day – not for 99.99% of the time. These days it is extremely difficult to find such a service.

Over 90% of all disappointed customers do not complain nor do they return.

5.1 On-line or manual

It is essential to access records and information quickly. Computer records should be instantaneous. Systems have been around for a long time now that can throw up customer and product information.

Employees referring to 'the computer' show a lack of perception of what is in the customer's mind. Mention of 'the computer' which may be blamed for foul-ups, pushes the personal touch one further step away from the customer. Whereas a customer can take an employee to task, thereby getting some satisfaction, a computer is a turn-off. The term 'we' or 'I' is preferable to the customer's ears. Computer systems that 'go down' or are inaccessible will kill your business. Try being personal; people like it. Take the service in a John Lewis store as an easy to observe example of what good service means.

A manual service, for example a two-person plumbing service, still needs to have information on continual access. Not knowing where the plumbers are, or the lack of essential information, will not recommend the service. A plumber who gets back to the customer within one hour with a time when he will call may encourage the customer to use his service.

5.2 Accuracy

Efficient systems only input information once. The information should be clear and concise. It should be right first time.

> I have seen a process of work involving customer orders, in a company with a turnover of £400 million, where the information was input twice at separate locations by different people. On top of this it was also partially changed or transferred three more times. Thousands of invoices were affected daily. All results were suspect.

If order processing people were shown the results of their work, i.e. how it affects the customer's business, especially when things don't go quite right, they would improve. This would mean that you would have to be prepared to take your people out to visit customers. This would have the effect of keeping a continuing dialogue going with the customers. It is essential to protect your bottom line right from the start. Customers are the bottom line.

The easiest way to communicate is to take the information customers give you and add as little as possible before representing it to them as an invoice. You may give their information more prominence on your invoices than you give your own products. This makes for more accuracy of information.

5.3 Credit trips

Credit trips are for the benefit of the customers to save them from their own indulgences and to safeguard company finances.

If you have a credit limit policy (and some companies do not) this should be made known to the customers. There are some companies that believe information such as customers' credit limits should never be divulged to customers. This concern is unnecessary. If the customers know the size of their credit limit that makes them feel someone is looking after their interests. Besides, most people in companies use credit cards that have credit limits. There is nothing negative in displaying credit limits.

You could get a situation where a customer gets someone in to look after the business while he takes holidays. The minder could make a mistake by adding several noughts to the order. A credit trip would throw out the order for closer inspection and consultation with the customer.

5.4 Order date versus delivery date versus invoice date

In an ideal world it would be nice for these events to happen on the same day. Often this is possible but not attempted. Should all of these documents get actioned on the same day, there is probably a better chance of the work being correct. This is basically because the order is fresh in people's minds. If something does go wrong, then if the company's documentation is all recognizable as same day material, it is easier to check and action.

Take an example of a newspaper advertisement, where all documents are actioned on different days. Customer complains.

Where is the paperwork – the order office, telesales, advertising, credit? But if, instead of this fiasco, there was only one document, which had one date and was dispatched to the customer on that date, how much easier life would be.

Order processing is not always about taking orders over the telephone or getting them through the mail. Take this example.

In the oil industry, there are those companies that pump the money in and those that pump the oil out.

The financiers like BP and Shell pay companies in the oil supply sector to get the oil. The oil supply companies make their money by supplying both the equipment (which they probably manufacture) and the experts, at daily rates. It is a volatile business. Losing an important contract or order may mean firing staff. Sometimes the number of staff fired might run to 90%. The experts move around companies. Many take their employees with them. They can be millionaires. No matter which company or group they join they jealously protect their corner. The difference between them and JR of *Dallas* fame is that, while they both eat meat, JR cooks his.

The experts are fiercely independent and they have a powerful sense of duty to each other when there is danger to life and limb.

One Monday morning I arrived for work to find my company was involved in rescuing a rig that had broken from its moorings in the Indian Ocean. The first few weeks' invoicing was going to amount to about $500,000 and I was having difficulties locating even one of the rig's numerous owners. I also had to find out how to send the primary documents (orders) to a floating rig, get them back, invoice them within a few days of the work being completed, in order to get paid within 30 days.

With the help of one of our experts we located one of the rig owners and by 12.30 p.m. met with his London representative to work out the finances. Another of the experts who was on his way through Heathrow Airport was briefed on the paperwork. This was a delicate operation, since he was flying out to a war zone to coordinate operations. And paperwork comes last.

The initial finances were through banker's draft. The order documentation was trickier, since any one route could not be relied upon for long. Orders were carried by hand and involved several couriers. Ships, planes and camels were used. Each order was required to be signed by the rig supervisor.

The rig was saved.

Figures 5.1, 5.2 and 5.3 show a bin card (for recording stock movements), order form/picking note and delivery note, respectively.

Product name					Bin no.				Reorder level		
Date	Ref.	Total stock			Stock allocated		Stock balance	Reorder		Period of days
		In	Out	Balance'	Qty	Date		Qty	Date	

Figure 5.1 Bin card for recording stock movements.

5.5 Summary

- Base systems and procedures (and have as few rules as possible) on customer requirement.

- Accuracy – get it right the first time, you might not get a second chance.

- React quickly – don't let the phones keep ringing. If people are good enough to contact your company you ought to be generous enough to make them feel they made the right decision and you deserve the call.

The Incredible Product Company PLC
Sleaseway Drive
Peterborough

Order Form
Picking Note

Customer Name and Address

Customer Number

Moveover Limited
High Street
Peterborough

89765

Page 1

Price	Product description	Product Code	Qty	Price	Product description	Product Code	Qty
	1 Car Product Range				2 DIY Clothes		
40.00	Fastlane horn	944	2	12.70	Slippers	212	20
200.00	Carphone	071	34	67.00	Overalls	213	
145.00	Blazesound	194	12	1.00	Socks, various	216	40
23.00	Autofax	674		12.00	Tool belt	219	
9.00	Nigel strip	754		15.00	Hard hat	234	
60.00	Squeal tyre	654		15.00	Miner's lamp	222	7
24.50	Strapins	578	4	4.00	Apron	225	
				5.00	Mittens	228	
	3 Videos			34.00	Rubber shoes	245	3
				3.00	Mouth mask	346	5
9.00	Out o'sight	323	9	34.00	Visor	348	3
9.00	Rubber ducks	341	3		4 Tapes		
9.00	Wally rides	343					
9.00	Son of Wally	348		6.99	Let's fly	425	
9.00	Gestures	350	9	6.99	High time	427	
9.00	Speed hogs	356		6.99	No waiting	431	17
9.00	Fluffy dice	357	2	6.99	Running in	433	7
9.00	Diced carrots	359	7	6.99	Route A6	434	2
9.00	Ducks' squeals	360	5	6.99	Can't stop	435	1
9.00	No minors	363	2	6.99	Got to be me	437	
9.00	Other cutups	367		6.99	Turnoff	439	
9.00	Hot rubber	368	7	6.99	944 special	440	3
9.00	Holdups	370		6.99	Gut Morgan	441	
9.00	Holdons	371	8	6.99	Red lights	443	
9.00	Famous skids	378	5	6.99	No lights	444	
9.00	Blind corners	379		6.99	What signals	445	4
				6.99	Blue lights	446	
	5 Garden			6.99	Horse power	447	
				6.99	Hearse power	448	
16.75	Plastic pots	502	2	6.99	High power	449	
21.50	Plastic seats	503	8	6.99	Contours	456	
16.79	Plastic statues	512		6.99	Closeness	457	
56.00	Plastic tables	521		6.99	Close enough	458	
3.50	Plastic buckets	524		6.99	Too close	459	

Figure 5.2 Order form/picking note.

HARRINGTON FOOD HALL LIMITED
Knightsbridge Green
London SW1

Mr John Pembleton-Smyth
87 Ovington Mews West
Knightsbridge
London SW1

DELIVERY NOTE NUMBER
0097

Customer A/C no.
P02435

Date   7 May 1990

Customer order no. telephone call today 4.46 p.m. Maria		
Quantity	**Product line**	**Description of product**
1	beverages	Head Waiter's Apple Juice

Dear Mr Pembleton-Smyth
This item will appear on your Invoice/Statement at the end of the current month

Thank you for your custom

Figure 5.3 Delivery note.

Cash Collection: Billing

Billing should be a simple process of advising the customer what goods/services have been supplied and when payment is expected.

The invoice may be the only legal document that passes between suppliers and customers. It is also an advertisement for the company. Its tone, how it looks, what message it gives influence what people do with it. And in the broader sense it influences how they feel about your company.

Do you speak the customer's language? If this is Italian, French or Spanish do you still invoice them in English? And, if so, think about the last time your purchase ledger assistant successfully handled an invoice from a Greek or Russian or Arabic supplier where they invoiced in their language. How long did it take you to pay the supplier?

What stops billing and the invoice from being a simple process for some companies is that the invoice is the creation of a number of people who each make a mark, whether this be a word, a line, or a feature, perhaps for their own internal purposes. The emphasis is taken off the customer at whom the invoice is aimed. This at times causes confusion in the customer's mind. Confusion can be caused by the simplest of omissions or an extra word in the wrong corner. A well-designed invoice can bring competitive advantage.

I have been able to improve the design of every invoice I have so far come across. The nearest I came to defeat was the invoice of an old established company in the construction business. The invoice had not been changed since its first showing in 1890. All I changed was the Shillings column (as in Pounds, Shillings and Pence). However, I have twice come across an invoice without the word invoice anywhere on the document.

An invoice has a legal status of up to seven years. However, this does not mean that you wait what you consider a reasonably genteel time before you prepare it and dispatch it. Companies fold up every day. Your customers are people like you who sometimes move on to new pastures and the personal continuity is disrupted. The sooner you send out invoices the sooner your customers will be able to deal with them. Give your customers the chance to comply with your terms of payment. Getting your invoices out in time is helping your customers to help you.

6.1 Terms of payment

Terms of payment are usually agreed by the board, who in some cases will consult with the credit manager. The credit manager is the company's expert on pitching the most effective terms. It makes for good management policy to consult the credit manager as part of the process of setting the terms so that he feels part of the decision-making process. He may then be more inclined to own the decision. This makes the manager more comfortable in administrating the terms.

Most companies will go along with payment terms normally accepted by the industry they are in.

Some companies may deliberately decide to give extended credit as part of their marketing strategy to win more customers. The extra cost to the company in bank interest charges must be taken into account. As it is a sales budget charge, this bank interest should be charged to the sales budget rather than to the credit department's budget. Appropriate allowances must be made in the credit department's figures when the credit period is worked out. It has been known for companies to overlook entirely the cost of extending credit.

Extended credit is not a good way of keeping or gaining customers. Here are four reasons why credit should be kept tight.

(1) Every day the debt is outstanding (your cash is in others' control) increases the chances of something nasty happening to it.

(2) Your service should be good enough to stand on its own. Allowing extra time to pay does not make it more efficient, or increase its quality. But it does allow your customers to become lazier, more relaxed and less financially efficient. On a wider scale, this encourages the industry to become less efficient.

(3) Credit managers watch the cash collection trends in the industry to compare their performances. It does not encourage them if they start from their point of view with their hands tied. It helps if the board recognizes and acknowledges the extra hurdle the manager has to face. However, if you allow extended terms, your credit manager will be seen as the least effective by the purchase ledger departments of your customers. This probably means that other correspondence, such as queries, are also handled relatively slowly. All in all you may be last everywhere.

(4) The longer it takes to collect your debts, the longer it takes you to react to the marketplace, especially if there is a sudden or unexpected change.

It is important how you word your terms of payment. Do you recognize these terms?

- '30 days net'
- '30 days from invoice date'

What message are these terms giving the customer? These terms are quite normally used and yet they should not be allowed to stand alone: 30 days net can be taken to mean that you pay on the 30th day without taking discount. But the 30th day of what? And there are people who might question what the word 'net' means. It is really not at all clear. Too much is left to the customer to read into the terms. Now '30 days from invoice day' is clearer but not by much. Presumably the terms do not mean that the customer is expected to get the cheque ready on the 30th day from the invoice day and then post it – perhaps by second class post. If such a payment was posted on a weekend it could in the end take an extra five days to reach the creditor.

Not everyone in the customer's purchase ledger department understands what a payment day is. Some will consider the account paid when they have passed the invoice on to the next stage. Yet this might be the first of many stages each invoice has to go through in order for payment to reach your account at the bank. You do not stand much chance of success if the customer's staff start to process the invoice for payment on the very day you expect to see the payment.

The following are more accurate messages to customers:

- 'Please pay within 30 days of the invoice date.'
- 'Please pay by 25th of the month following the month of invoice.'
- 'Please ensure that your payment reaches this office by 24 August 1990.'

The difference between both sets of terms of payment is that the latter three are more polite, more accurate and they ask for money sooner. Generally, the last three are more customer friendly and project a higher professional image.

Do people notice the payment terms?

> The first time I managed to get the word 'please' into the terms of payments I had four customers ring up with very pleasant comments.
>
> It pays to try to improve a service. The improvement is not always appreciated, but it is nice when some recognition is voiced. People do notice.

It is quite common to find the payment terms requesting payment by the end of the month following the month of invoice. This is sometimes inaccurately described as '60 day' terms. The thinking here is that an invoice dated 1 November will not be due for payment until 31 December, hence 60 days. However, this thinking forgets that all invoices in the current month are due for payment at the end of the following month. This averages 45 days (an average of 15 days in the current month plus 30 days in the second month).

Most companies in the United Kingdom divide their year into 12 calendar sales periods. Working on terms of payment that expect payment at the same time as everyone else and at the busiest time of the month is not good strategy. Therefore, the terms of payment already mentioned above offer a more favourable route to better payment.

By allowing customers more time than they need to sell your stock you are funding their business at the expense of your own. You are also taking greater risks than you need or intend to. That is not what most companies go into business to do. That is the business of banks.

So, payment terms should be precise, give a clear message and be relevant to the business you are in.

6.2 Discount

TRADE DISCOUNT

Trade discount is a marketing decision, based on market forces, and is not normally the concern of the credit manager. However, credit managers are aware of the impact trade discount can have on their customers, the market and the industry they are in. And although trade discount is a fact of normal commercial and industrial life it does have, when allowed, one huge disadvantage: it does away with effective competition, i.e. volume discount to large organizations puts smaller ones at a disadvantage and can put them out of business altogether.

Industries that suffer from lack of competition because of large trade discounts, like the food and record industries, tend to get lazy. This results in higher prices without any further benefit to the end consumer. As the players in the marketplace become fewer and fewer so they are able to dictate more and more to the market.

This affects the suppliers and the consumers equally. The suppliers' margins are cut to the bone and they have to take short cuts. Quality suffers. The consumer suffers. This does not just affect the individual supplier, or a few customers and one or two end consumers. Since most suppliers in some industries, the food and record industries, to name only two, are in the business of volume discount it affects the whole industry. And since most industries work on trade discount, a something-for-nothing thinking process prevails.

Volume discount can sometimes appear to get out of hand. In the construction industry, for example, nails can be discounted at between 70 and 80%. In the food business volume discounting produces, at best, bland food and little choice for the consumer. At its worst, it can lead to dangerous short cuts in food quality. In the record industry volume discount leads to old hits being revived at the expense of new material, simply because it is easier.

Trade discounts mean blandness.

CASH SETTLEMENT DISCOUNT

Cash settlement discount is a good tool to use in trying to tighten cashflow. It must be an advantage to collect money sooner, with less effort. Obviously the gain to the customers is that they get the goods at a lower price. The supplier passes on the saving in bank interest to the customer.

An important aspect of this discount is that when it works properly it keeps the whole process lean and mean, without affecting quality. Suppliers who can count on being paid quickly can plan more easily with a safer cashflow.

There are, however, sometimes elementary mistakes made when allowing cash settlement discount.

- If your terms of payment state that you would like payment by the end of the month following the month of invoice, there is not much point allowing 'cash settlement discount for paying on or before the 30th of the month following the month of invoice'. Yet this is not an uncommon mistake.

- You can make a statement of intent – 'cash settlement discount of 2½% will be allowed if payment is received by the 10th of the month following the month of invoice' – and monitor the payments carelessly.

    This could lead to a situation arising where you (i) do not get the benefits of early cashflow, (ii) still have to pay the bank charges and (iii) have disagreements with customers on a secondary problem (cash settlement discount) that does not involve product quality and is a little removed from the main source of income and reason for being in business.

Sometimes the question of cash settlement can go to people's heads, or to be more accurate over their heads. Take the following example:

> In my capacity as a credit manager in the music industry, I once received through the post an invitation to reply immediately to one of our customer's requests for preferential cash settlement terms.
>
> The letter clearly indicated that the customer would not buy from us unless we agreed to the terms of the letter. The customer, a big London store, which no longer exists, put forward the following terms:
>
> (1) 2½% cash settlement for payment by the 30th of the month following the month of invoice;
> (2) 3¼% CSD for payment in one week;
> (3) 5% CSD for payment by return.
>
> I reviewed the account. The store's payment record was not the best. It normally paid late and deducted the discount. There was evidence of correspondence and phone calls each month to recover the discount. This meant that it could not keep to the current CSD terms.
>
> I looked at the store's method of processing payments. Putting this into the context of its being able to fulfil its new schedule I came up with the following timetable:
>
> - Mail received and passed to purchase ledger department on same day.
> - Invoices then internally dated and sent to music buyer on day two.
> - Music buyer would tie up the invoice and the delivery note, sign the invoice for payment and pass to purchase ledger next day, day three.
> - Purchase ledger would pass the invoice for payment and request a cheque from the chief accountant's office, which they would expect to receive the following day, when they would post it to us.
> - If it was sent first class post the earliest the cheque would reach us would be on the eighth day (since included in the calculation

is a weekend and the initial day when we posted the invoice to the store).

In addition, I checked with its purchase ledger department and was able to confirm that all the mail was sent second class. This would obviously add another day. In other words the letter's implications for others was not thought through very carefully.

I did not really have to do any of this investigation for my own benefit. But I would have to explain to the sales department as well as my superiors that as the customer could not possibly achieve the terms in the letter my advice was to pass over the invitation. Having got all-round agreement I contacted the customer's MD, who immediately withdrew the letter.

It turned out to be the idea of one person in the customer's accounts department who obviously could not have foreseen the consequences.

Cash settlement discount must be monitored to make sure that the benefits that are planned to accrue do so. One way to achieve this is for the credit manager to get involved at an early stage of a new account. The customer must be made aware that discount is a two-way benefit and not something that can be taken for granted.

6.3 The invoice

The invoice is the most important document a company will normally send out. The next person to get it is the customer. For this reason it must appear customer friendly. The payment terms should contain the word please. Every effort should be made to get it right first time. The spelling of the names of customer's staff should be correct. Where possible first names should be used.

A well-designed invoice can be an advertisement in itself.

THE INVOICE DESIGN

The essential items of information required on an invoice are given in Figure 6.1 and may be enumerated as follows:

(1) The word 'invoice'

(2) Your name and address

(3) Amount due

(4) Date of invoice

(5) Invoice number

(6) Customer's name and address

(7) Terms of payment

(8) Description of debt, including itemized charges and VAT (sales tax)

(9) Customer's reference, and date of order, and their account number for you

(10) Your references, including account number and delivery note references (the numbers should be the same)

(11) VAT number

(12) Telephone number

(13) Fax number

In some sales ledger systems, invoices have the word 'invoice' buried somewhere among the boxes. This kind of invoice design pays more attention to aesthetics than to the main purpose for which it was intended.

In any document the eye will be drawn to the right (perhaps it is the way we read and write that accounts for this, but if you want to get noticed in a photograph get on the left of the others or the right side as one looks at the picture). An invoice should have the word 'invoice', the invoice number and the date in the top right-hand corner. When you have to find a hard-copy invoice it is much easier thumbing through paper where the invoice number is in the top right-hand corner (see Figure 6.1).

It is worth remembering that the customers will have a supplier's account number for you. Quoting this number prominently could get you further up the line of being paid than your competitors.

Address details that may sometimes get missed are post codes – yours and your customers. Missing the post code could delay payments being received by two to three days.

O'SULLIVANS WINES

INVOICE

Arsenal FC
Highbury
London
NW1 XXX

A/C No   OS 8976

INVOICE NO
4876
INVOICE DATE
2 MAY 1989
A/C NO
342

Customer Order Number A41921	**Date of order** 2 May 1989

Description of goods supplied			£
Quantity	Type		
200	wine	Red French various (as per enclosed list)	900.00
200	wine	White French/German (as per enclosed list)	1500.00
		Congratulations	
		Goods amount	2400.00
		Total VAT	360.00
		TOTAL INVOICE AMOUNT	£ 2760.00

TERMS OF PAYMENT   Please pay within 30 days of invoice date

O'Sullivans Wines   **45 Highbury Street London NW1 XXX**
Tel 071–000–0000   Fax 071–000–0000
VAT Registration Number 000000000000

Figure 6.1 Invoice.

The position of the company's name on the invoice can be important. When invoices are clipped, stapled or held together, the usual place this is done is in the left-hand corner of the document. Therefore, if your company name is in the top left-hand corner it will be hard to find when flicking through the paperwork. You could make it easier for your customers by centring the name for easy finding.

Common faults in invoice design are:

- Confused message or too many messages.

- Too many words.

- Too many lines and boxes. When invoices are designed by committee they run the risk of everyone having a line or box inserted to keep everyone happy. The invoice takes on an internal look with boxes in some cases for 'office use only'.

- No space or obscure place for customer reference. One customer reference normally forgotten is their account number for you. If you include this they will find your account faster.

- Some terms of payment are not properly understood. For example the word 'net' is sometimes not understood by the personnel of the companies who use the term. The word 'strictly' is not customer friendly and is in any case superfluous. You should expect customers to pay with pleasure and not strictly.

- Invoice number not emphasized.

- Invoice date not emphasized.

- Confused financial advice.

6.4 The statement

The question is often asked whether statements are necessary. Traditionally, the statement is used to give customers a monthly look at how their account stands. And it also acts as a reminder of how much they owe. There are two kinds of statement: the brought forward statement and the open item statement.

(1) The B/F statement shows a list of the current month's items in between a balance total brought forward from the previous month and the new total which includes the current items. Because the B/F statement just totals previous months, it is not helpful to see the picture of where the account stands. Reconciling statements can, therefore, sometimes be troublesome. This may not be the image you might want to give customers. These statements are being phased out. If you are unfortunate to have inherited a B/F system, have it replaced immediately, before you lose more customers. B/F statements are harmful to cash collection.

(2) The open item statement shows all outstanding items and so gives a clear picture to the customer of what is being claimed as owed.

Some large-volume customers normally do not look at statements. These customers just pay the invoices as they come in. If it is known that a customer does not want a statement, the statement should be kept back. However, if this customer does not pay to terms or has missed payment on a number of invoices then sending a statement pointing out the outstanding invoices would help to pinpoint the message.

The individual attention you can give customers depends on the volume of statements, the number of people you employ to look after the accounts, the industry you are in and the way you do things. Generally, most customers will want statements.

Normally the question of whether or not to send out statements is asked because someone is looking at the possibility of saving money on (i) printing costs, (ii) labour costs, (iii) computer costs or (iv) postage costs.

The only issue is whether the customers want the service. If you are not sure, and you are thinking about a change, ask them. If, by taking a view and without asking the customers, you stop sending out statements, and as a result you lose one customer, will the exercise have been worth it?

Since statements remind customers of their outstanding debt to you, their use to the credit department is to act as a cash collection tool. Any aid to cash collection should not be given up without some hard thinking.

THE STATEMENT DESIGN

The essential items of information required on a statement are given in Figure 6.2 and may be enumerated as follows:

(1) The word 'statement'

(2) Your name and address and telephone number

(3) Date of statement

(4) Total amount due

(5) Amount overdue

(6) Customer's name and address

(7) Account number

(8) Terms of payment

(9) Itemized list of references, i.e. invoices, credit notes, debit notes, cash, etc., brief description plus customer's reference number

(10) VAT number

(11) Fax number

(12) Telex number

Common faults in statement design are:

• One mistake frequently made is to include an aged debt at the foot of the statement. This encourages customers to pay later. Here is an example of such an aged debt:

| Current | Overdue | | | | Total |
month	1–30	31–60	61–90	90⁺	Due

What this is saying to a customer is 'Look here, you are not doing so badly. Some of our customers wait until they get invoices in the last box category before they pay. Why else would we show all these boxes?'

O'SULLIVANS WINES

		STATEMENT

Arsenal FC
Highbury
London
NW1 XXX

STATEMENT

31 MAY 1989

A/C NO

A/C No   OS 8976

342

Customer Date ref.	Our Date ref.	Brief description of goods supplied	Over-due 0	£
A41917 1-5-89	i4866 1-5-89	Soft drinks		360.00
A41921 2-5-89	i4876 2-5-89	Wine		2760.00
A41929 7-5-89	i4921 7-5-89	Soft drinks		400.00
A41937 15-5-89	i4964 15-5-89	Soft drinks		180.00

TOTAL AMOUNT DUE   £3700.00

TERMS OF PAYMENT   Please pay within
30 days of invoice date

O'Sullivans Wines   **45 Highbury High Street London NW1 XXX**
Tel 071–000–0000   Fax 071–000–0000
VAT Registration Number 000000000000

Figure 6.2 Statement showing essential information.

- Customer references are put in as an afterthought. These references are how the customer will recognize the debt in the first instance. Therefore, it makes sense to use this as the basis of the reminder.
- Too many lines, boxes and words.

6.5 Volumes

Statements will be produced on the night or day following the last invoice day. They should be presented to the customers, within two to three days from the month end, or by the very latest in the first week of the new month.

It would certainly help if the sales and, therefore, the invoices were evenly spread throughout the month. Some companies are apparently slow to make sales early in the month but seem always to catch up in the last few days just before the cut-off stage at month end. This places enormous strain on resources at a particularly difficult time in the month. The result may very well be seen in delayed end-of-month figures. This in itself is not important. What is important is that this delays forecasting the next month's operational goals.

The credit manager, who is at the sharp end of this practice, should be able to question why sales are not well planned or why the sales department is more bound by the end-of-month targets as against serving the customers all the time. On occasion, concentrating on the end-of-month goal may be the only way to motivate the sales team. It is noticeable that when the sales team is monitored closely throughout the month the sales are spread more evenly.

6.6 Summary

- Keep your customers' minds concentrated on paying your invoices. That is the reason you send them out.

- Give them the very best information to help them. Keep it simple, clear and friendly.
- Getting it right at the invoice stage is the first step in the cash collection effort.

Cash Collection: Getting Ready

If you prepare well you should do well. In terms of cash collection preparing well means getting as much information about customers as is possible. When you get to the stage where you are explaining their systems to them, you can feel that you are getting there.

If you can offer them something more than other competitors for their money then you are further along the line. Doing what you promise inspires their confidence in you. Simple promises of action could be: calling them back within a set time limit; getting the credit note to them 'by Tuesday'; having a word with your sales director about discounts; making sure that your company's deliveries to their main works arrive on a certain day of the week; giving their queries top priority, and letting them know that you will always do so; helping them to get your paperwork through their system. The more they rely on you the stronger the business relationship will become. This safeguards your operation.

You will need to monitor how you do it. How do you keep tabs on whether you always ring back when you say you will? How do you know or remember whether the customer was satisfied with your answer on discounts? Did you subsequently check on whether your carriers are now delivering product to the customer's satisfaction? How many of these promises are converted into positive results? How does all this affect the DSO for instance? You will need a monitoring system.

7.1 A suggested system

Any system should have a strategy. The starting point for this particular system could be to improve the DSO (the credit period).

To do this it is necessary to monitor how the customer's accounts are currently being serviced. This kind of information is more accurately established by recording the details of contact with customers. What are customers saying? Do we need to take any action? Have we taken any action? Are we learning from our previous mistakes? Where should our priorities lie? Accurate monitoring is essential, since all analysis and action that follows would be wasted if we went down the wrong paths.

Any monitoring system should be action biased. Otherwise it will not work. If there is no obligation on individuals (including members of the board of directors) to act on the information, they will tend not to do so. Customers' comments should not be hidden away in files. The comments should get into the mainstream of the business quickly, before anyone can change or dilute the content. Information time-lags cost money. Obviously any system should be customer orientated, since it starts and ends with the customer, i.e. the customer orders and the customers pays.

The more experience you gain in information gathering the more you will see how it can be used to improve the everyday running of the business. The information will highlight how to deal with customers in a way they will more readily accept. Planning what you have to do each month to improve your results should become clearer. Forecasting your cashflow should become more accurate.

Whether you use the suggested system as a manual operation or computerize it (and there are computerized systems that can incorporate much of what is here, though by no means all of it) depends on your own set of circumstances. The system that is described in this chapter can be contained in a lever-arch folder. This can sit neatly on a desk, preferably beside the telephone and a diary.

It can form part of an integrated system on cash collection

and customer after-sales service that is described throughout the book.

7.2 Collecting information

It is sometimes forgotten that the most accurate information on customers comes from customers. In order to capture it for future use and to monitor what has happened there are three forms suggested (see Figures 7.1, 7.2 and 7.3).

- Customer contact details record (Figure 7.1)
  One of these should be used for each customer. It records essential details and other details sometimes overlooked but vital to effective cash collection. The kind of details to record here are:

  - How do they pay?
  - What is their system?
  - How is the paperwork handled?
  - Who are the people involved, i.e. who signs the cheques?

  Other details that you discover from time to time, like birthdays, where they live (perhaps, if it comes up in conversation, they could live in your street), what their kids do (I discovered for example that one purchase manager's daughter worked for me). Since you will deal with some customers perhaps more frequently than with people in your own company, you may even strike up friendships with them that go through your entire business life. Instead of treating every meeting with customers as a ritual confrontation you could look forward to visiting them in their own towns.

- Customer conversation details record (Figure 7.2)
  If you keep a record as brief as you can to recall what customers say, you will notice that they will run out of excuses as you continually recite the things they have said previously. To be kind to the customers, what is an invalid excuse to you may sound and be very reasonable to them. We may all be under

---

CUSTOMER CONTACT DETAILS

Customer Name . . . .

ours for them   theirs for us

Account Number . . . .

Telephone Number . . . .

Invoice Address   Statement Address

. . . .

. . . .

. . . .

. . . .

Contacts

                Name   Position   Ext

. . . .

. . . .

. . . .

. . . .

. . . .

Notes on Payment

_____

_____

_____

_____

_____

_____

_____

_____

_____

_____

Figure 7.1 Customer contact details.

pressure sometimes and may like to put off action for another time. This does not help the cash collection effort.

So to recap, this record helps:

- customers' memories;
- you to concentrate on the things that matter, i. e. the future;

CUSTOMER NAME		A/C NO	
DATE	CONTACT	REMARKS	

Use diary for follow-up dates

Figure 7.2 Customer conversation details.

- when the individual staff member is away on holidays the holiday cover person can just take over knowing that all the necessary information is available.

Where you need to call a customer again you can make a note in your diary. To save paper you can use both sides of the form.

- Customer daily contact sheet record (Figure 7.3)
This sheet is kept as the flyleaf of the lever-arch folder. It is used for recording the number of conversations you have each day with customers. It does not matter if you call them or they call you, as long as you spoke to the customer's contact.

  This reminds you of the volume of customer contact you had throughout the month. The credit manager can gauge whether:

  - there were enough calls (as per the plan);
  - how effective these calls were (by the individual's results) and can obviously refer to how the calls progressed by looking up the customer conversation details record.
  Holiday cover can also see at a glance who was called.
  Obviously both sides of the form can be used.

7.3 Setting targets

In order to be able to relieve customers of their money at a quick enough pace to keep your company in business, you need to formulate a plan. The plan should be simple and clear enough for staff to follow and for management to monitor. The plan should be achievable and realistic.

But what are you capable of and what should you concentrate on? Management normally concentrates on the number of days it takes you to collect amounts outstanding.

THE CREDIT PERIOD OR DAYS' SALES OUTSTANDING (DSO)

There are numerous and wonderful ways of arriving at a figure by which the credit department's performance is judged. The

DATE	A/C No.	ACCOUNT NAME	DATE	A/C No.	ACCOUNT NAME

Figure 7.3 Customer daily contact sheet.

three most common are 2M, 3M, and the exhaust method. Each method can give a different answer. This is how they work.

Take sales figures for the last three months as January £1000, February £1250 and March £1500. Take a balance on the sales ledger or accounts receivable as £3200.

(1) Calculation of the 2M method:

$$\frac{\text{March outstanding balance}}{\text{Last two months' sales}} \times 60$$

$$= \frac{3200}{2750} \times 60 = 69.8 \text{ or } 70 \text{ days}$$

(2) Calculation of the 3M method:

$$\frac{\text{March outstanding balance}}{\text{Last three months' sales}} \times 90$$

$$= \frac{3200}{3750} \times 90 = 76.8 \text{ or } 77 \text{ days}$$

(3) Calculation of the exhaust method:

			Days
March balance outstanding	3200		
Less current month's sales	1500	=	31
	1700		
Less February sales	1250	=	28
	450		
Remainder as a proportion of January sales, i.e. (450/1000) × 31 = 13.9		=	14
			73 days

Therefore, to recap on the three methods

Calculation using the 2M method	DSO	=	70 days
Calculation using the 3M method	DSO	=	77 days
Calculation using the exhaust method	DSO	=	73 days

Which one to select? In this example the 2M method seems to give the best result. However, in practice it evens out much more.

The 2M method is the two months' method. Each month is considered 30 days, which is why the equation is multiplied by 60: 30 + 30 = 60.

3M is the three months' method. The reason why there are two methods is partly traditional. The assumption is that 2M is used mainly for UK business on the basis that UK payment terms are 60 day terms and that overseas terms are 90 days. Neither of these assumptions is correct.

In addition, the calculation is misleading. Multiplying 30 × 12 or 90 × 4 works out at 360 days. However, there are 365 days in the year. Therefore, as an exact figure it is incorrect.

The exhaust method has two immediately easy to see advantages over the other two. Firstly, it counts 365 days in the year; therefore it is more accurate and correct. Secondly, it is current, taking the most recent month's figures into account. A further advantage is that it is easier to explain because it is more logical.

Still, there are lots more ingenious and complicated methods used. The trouble is that each company may have a policy of using one particular method. This particular method may have no relevance to the marketplace but because the company is multinational it will not change just for you. The assumption here is that anything is all right as long as the same yardstick is used each time. This is, of course, invalid.

In one company I came across the DSO was being calculated on 260 days in the year. The reason behind this calculation was very clear. The credit manager only worked from Monday to Friday, i.e. five days per week, and to be fair to him the company only calculated the DSO using the working days in the year: 5 × 52 = 260. The logic took no account of the manager's annual holidays, bank holidays and sick leave and other seemingly irrelevant facts such as outside comparisons and bank charges.

I understand the frustration of some managers I come across, seeing what is to be done but not having enough influence to be able to do anything about it. Then out of the blue comes a consultant who is about to take up the same banner. How frustrating.

Normally when I notice things that are not correct I will first pass on the news to the person who has got it wrong. If he subsequently changes the bad practice, which no one else has noticed, then as far as I am concerned it is good for him and it makes my job easier. There will be no need for me to pass on news of this incident to anyone else.

I see my job as helping the client and this means all members of the client's team. My motivation is seeing something work better. I expect all praise for a job well done to go to the team. The team have to keep the show going after I've gone. When my client's employees feel better about themselves, I know the board will be satisfied.

Like everyone else I sometimes put my foot in it. Don't get me wrong. I don't mind making a fool of myself while I'm being paid. But the biggest gaffe I can make when starting a credit project is to embarrass a client's credit manager.

On one particular occasion I was very optimistic about being able to help. Here I was, having been introduced to the client on a project which was to do with a few days' workshop training. I discovered that the administration was so overloaded with unnecessary duplication that I saw a whole lengthy project rising up beckoning me.

Somehow we got around to talking about DSO. I told the story about the 260 day year where they only counted the working days. I was asked about it at length while someone went off to get the figures. I was handed the figures while we were talking. To my alarm and horror I discovered that they were calculated on 260 days.

When the annual figures are published the competition, along with the City, etc., will calculate the DSO by dividing debtors by sales multiplied by 365.

So now you have to decide whether you can better last month's performance for the month of April. You will also need to calculate how much money you need to collect. Assume that you are using the exhaust method of calculation and you want to achieve an improvement of three days to reduce the DSO to 70 days. The sales department gives you a sales forecast of £1900 for April.

The calculation follows:

March balance outstanding	£3200	=	73	DSO
Plus April sales	1900	=	30	DSO
	5100	=	103	DSO
1 day = 49.5 (5100/103)				
70 days (49.5 × 70)	3465	(April balance)		
Cash to collect	1635			

The sales ledger balance you are forecasting as outstanding for April is £3465 and in setting yourself a cash collection target of 70 DSO, you will try to collect £1645. (Figure 7.4 shows where the sales forecast fits into the monthly report.)

When setting the targets you should take into account information you already possess that will affect the outcome. For example, if you are having trouble with a large account that will not be resolved until the following month, this may impact on your basic assumptions. Perhaps you are aware that the sales effort in March contained an element of extended credit. This might result in a one-month delay in payment on, say, 50% of March sales.

Are you making comparisons with other companies in the same industry to see where your track record stands? No credit manager can get complacent. A company merger might mean the new organization having to choose between two credit managers. But if you are doing better than others in the same industry don't be shy about the word getting out in your own outfit. You can even get this into your monthly report.

DEBTORS AGED LISTING REPORT

This report will form the basis of the credit department's monthly management report.

Most computerized systems' aged debts are in five categories: current, and overdue (1–30 days, 31–60 days, 61–90 days. and 91 days and over). Each account takes up one line which includes a total.

The listing enables the credit manager to quickly review the sales ledger. However, no report should be read in isolation. For instance, if there is a problem on cash allocation, where the cash

SALES OUTSTANDING AGED ANALYSIS REPORT   Period_____

Month	Actual Sales	DSO Actual	DSO Plan
Mar			
Apr			
May			
June			
Jul			
Aug			
Sept			
Oct			
Nov			
Dec			
Jan			
Feb			
Mar			

Month	3 Month Forecast DSO	3 Month Forecast S/L Bal	COMMENT
Mar			
Apr			
May			
June			
July			
Aug			
Sept			
Oct			
Nov			
Dec			
Jan			
Feb			
Mar			

See text for notes on report calculations and on terms used

Figure 7.4 Where the sales forecast fits into the monthly report.

is dumped in the current category the credit manager will have to adjust the balances in each category accordingly to get a clear picture. He can then take a view on which accounts to target during the month.

The most important figure on each line of the aged listing is the total. Taking the totals and placing them in order of importance by value enables a further zeroing in on the monthly target. There are a few ways to do this. One of these is a simple format of the sales ledger balance summary.

CUSTOMER PROFILE/SALES LEDGER BALANCE SUMMARY

This format (see Figure 7.5) can show account number/name and a number of categories of account values, with a space for comments. The idea is to isolate the high-value accounts so that these are reviewed first. The value of each balance will appear in the space under the appropriate category. The accounts appear in alphabetical order.

For example, in a high-value, low-volume market where there are, say, 250 customers the number of sheets needed to target the accounts would be six. The first category might start at £100,000 + , the second could include accounts with balances of £50,000–100,000, and so on.

This might seem to ignore the slow paying and low-value accounts. But in targeting to affect cashflow, these low-value accounts do not count for much against recent high-value and easier to collect accounts. Low-value accounts are covered later in the book.

CASH COLLECTION TARGET SHEET

The cash collection target sheet (see Figure 7.6) is designed to give a complete up-to-date picture on the progress of cash collection throughout the month. It is literally up to the minute.

The 'Cash in' column shows the total amount of cash received in the day. Each day's cash receipts are totalled and entered each day in the 'Total cash in to date' box. The balance between this figure and the 'Cash target' figure is the new outstanding balance to collect to meet the monthly target.

NO.	NAME	10K+	5K–10K	1K–5K	500 to 1K	100 to 500	Up to 100	Comment

Figure 7.5 Sales ledger balance summary.

DAY	CASH IN	CASH PROMISED		
		CUSTOMER'S NAME	AMOUNT	DATE
1				
2				
3				
4				
5				
6				
7				
8				
9				
10				
11				
12				
13				
14				
15				
16				
17				
18				
19				
20				
21				
22				
23				
24				
25				
26				
27				
28				
29				
30				
31				

CASH TARGET £_____

TOTAL CASH IN TO DATE

DATE	£

NOTES

Figure 7.6 Cash collection target sheet.

The 'Cash promised' column is for actual promises by customers, and includes a space to record the amount promised and the date that you expect to see the payment. The total figure in this column can then temporarily be subtracted from the cash target. Among the notes you could have amounts that you would normally expect to see on particular dates without a phone call or promise from customers.

What you are continually doing throughout the month is zeroing in on the amounts you have got to collect to meet the corporate cash collection target.

7.4 Summary

- The fitter and more prepared you are the more you will enjoy what you do.

- One alternative to not having a plan each month is to come in each day, pick up the nearest piece of paper, whatever its importance, and get on with the day. If this happens in your department it probably happens in the other departments too. Is this any way to run a business?

- Having the right tools to do the job is an essential part of cash collection. Planning the collection target is providing the will. Building up your cash mountain and seeing the gap between forecast and actual cash received diminish each day keeps the plan alive. It also keeps the company alive.

Cash Collection: Getting Paid

8.1 Communication

The essential skill required in cash collection is the skill to communicate effectively. This must be backed up by the will to communicate constantly each day. Good communication is not just about imparting information, it is about listening. In fact the best communicator is the one who listens first.

The ability to listen enables credit personnel to establish a sound understanding of customer needs. This understanding is crucial before deciding on what action to take. Since the job requires that decisions are made constantly throughout each day by first-level staff, decisions that can affect the future of the company's business relationship with customers, it must be explained to these personnel what is expected of them and how to achieve these expectations.

There is sometimes to be heard among managers the apparent willingness to put customers first. This is to be applauded. Unfortunately in some instances they have no idea what this means. How many managers think the customer is always right, or that the customer pays their salaries? How many would give up a weekend to help a customer? How many answer the phone on the first ring or always ring back when they promised? How many managers have actually met their customers at the customers' premises?

I know of one instance where a consultant was usually greeted by the head office managers meeting group of a major travel company with nonchalant statements like 'our customers always come first'. This was in contrast to the consultant's reading of events. His review revealed that the managers had basically lost touch with the branch offices that dealt with customers.

Abandonding the understanding of what customers want to branch offices or junior personnel is to lose a grip on the business. In credit management terms even a slight relaxation of that grip could prove fatal to a company. The credit department looks after the most valuable company assets: customers and their money.

8.2 Credit manager's main task

The primary function of the credit manager is to collect the company's debts within the terms of payment. How this is carried out can be of tremendous interest to all company departments.

To have an effective means of actioning customer requests, the credit department must have access to some means of getting adequate response from other company departments. This is covered fully in Chapter 10. Such a control must be supported by senior management by being continually monitored. It demonstrates how customer queries can be actioned by all company departments.

The credit manager's main aim can be somewhat diluted by introducing very simple innocent-looking procedures. These start by asking the manager for more detailed reports on late payers and progress to the point where the monthly report starts to concentrate on the bad debts side of the business.

In the context of cash collection, there are two categories of accounts – those accounts that are not yet due for payment and those that are overdue. The emphasis in this chapter is on keeping all the accounts current.

8.3 Payment and collection cycles

In some companies the first call on a customer for payment of the account, following dispatch of invoices and the statement, is when the account is overdue for payment. Obviously this is too late.

If experience shows that a number of customers, as yet not identified, pay late each month, it must make sense to try and identify the reasons why this is so. Therefore, the alternative to calling them after the horse has bolted is to call while the going is good, i.e. before the account becomes overdue for payment.

Some companies call their customers up to a week before the account is due for payment. This alerts the customers to the money owed and the obligation to pay. It gives customers a chance to pay within payment terms. Those credit departments who call up to one week before payment is due are trying harder to safeguard their company's debts. But they could do better.

Maybe taking the example of the purchase ledger system in your own company you can determine the length of time it takes to process suppliers' invoices. You can compare this with, say, ten customer systems. Now perhaps you have discovered that invoices are on average processed every nine days. Therefore, by the tenth day the customers will know when the invoices are scheduled to be paid. Might it not be prudent to call the customers on the tenth day?

The idea of calling customers on the tenth day, as against one week before the accounts are due for payment, achieves two objectives. The first will confirm the payment position and also whether the cashflow forecast is on schedule. The second will confirm whether the customers are happy with your products and service.

In the long run, if the customers are not happy with your service, you will not get paid and your cashflow will not remain protected. Therefore, the main aim of the customer contact should shift towards reaffirming customer satisfaction. This leans more towards an after-sales service (what is becoming known as customer care). It is far better that you find out at an early stage whether customers are satisfied with your products and service, than for your competitors to find out through customers' frustrations.

By calling customers early you will be able to avert difficulties that they would have encountered had you waited for the normal bureaucratic process to run its course. You will also, by coincidence, be in a better position to be able to help them to meet your payment terms.

Were you to adopt an after-sales service approach towards customers, you would have to alter slightly your relationship with your customers' purchase ledger departments. Since part of this service would necessitate your going through to other customer departments to review individual cases of dissatisfaction and then reporting progress to the purchase ledger department, you would seem to be performing part of the latter's function. If you tackle it correctly and with respect for the customers' internal departments, you will achieve your goals.

Basically what you would be doing is reacting quickly to the marketplace. Your approach will help the rest of your company to react faster and, more importantly, in a more individual and personal way to customers. And that in modern UK will give you a competitive edge.

It is surprising what you can discover when reviewing your own company systems, especially the ones whose aim is to respond to customers. Even the simplest processes may be capable of improvement. Take the following example.

It does help if you can get the simple things right.

A pharmaceutical company with a number of offices in the same town, traditionally had its mail for three offices delivered by the Royal Mail to one of these offices. The schedule seemed to be that the mail was delivered to office A for internal distribution to offices B and C.

I couldn't see any advantage to the company in these arrangements, so I visited mail receptions in offices B and C and the mailroom in office A.

I discovered that the mail collection programme was not working to plan. The mail picked up by the internal service from office A for delivery to offices B and C turned out to be the previous day's mail. This was because the internal service van only did one mail run each morning, and that started before office A had time to sort out that day's mail. In the afternoon it only collected the outgoing mail.

In other words the mail for offices B and C arrived a day late. This had a significant impact on customer orders. But from the credit manager's point of view the cheques arrived one day late. This obviously affected performance. More importantly customers were being called to pay accounts when the money 'was in the post'.

Office A was also responsible for sending out the mail. In terms of the credit department this included invoices and statements. I further discovered that the envelopes in which the statements were mailed were held up for 4/5 days while advertising literature was enclosed. This seemed a curious advertising strategy. The envelope would get opened by either a buyer or the purchase ledger department. Each would have no interest in the other's literature. In all probability they would drop the other's mail in the waste bin. Each would have wondered what the supplier was up to. It must have been confusing at times.

The effect of the delay in sending out the statements was also to hold up the dispatch of the invoices by 4/5 days.

In total the setback in the cycle of cash collection to the credit department was at least 5 days per month. No credit department deserves to be put under such a handicap.

Concentrating on getting the simple things right helps.

8.4 Cash collection comparison

Where you put the emphasis on the cash collection effort will depend on your overall company culture.

A customer-orientated culture would put the emphasis up front. A middle of the road culture, with no particular emphasis, might start the collection process with ten days to go before the due payment date. Then there is the crisis driven culture where everything is always done in a hurry at the last minute.

Logically the sooner you react the sooner things happen. Also the sooner you react the more time you have to get things right. The amount of effort you put into it is another factor. But this is not affected by when you start the process of cash collection. In other words, you could put the same amount of effort into the after-sales service method as into a method that is mainly geared to overdue debts. An ever increasing element of the latter method is the involvement of outside debt collection agencies.

In the everyday routine of the credit department you could spot the difference between the way the two methods work. The activity generated by the after-sales service method is geared towards help with product and customer-related items. Talk and action will revolve around getting things done, encouraging internal departments and reporting progress to customers. In contrast, in the chasing of money method, talk and action will

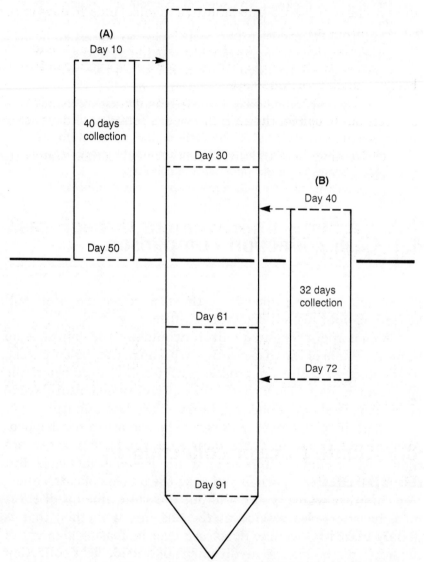

Terms of payment – Please pay by 20th of month following month of invoice.

Figure 8.1 Comparison of monthly routine (A) and cash chasing method (B).

revolve around invoices, aged debt listings and debt collection agencies.

In Figure 8.1 there is a comparison of the monthly routine and the cash chasing method.

The payment terms mean that the DSO target is 35 days. This figure is arrived at by taking an average invoice time of 15 days in the first month (the month of invoice) plus 20 days in the month following the month of invoice.

The after-sales service method starts to call customers on day 10 and sets out to collect the accounts over a period of 40 days before reaching the due date.

The cash chasing method starts to call customers on day 40 and sets out to collect the accounts over a period of 11 days before reaching the due date.

Quite obviously the after-sales service method stands the best chance of success.

8.5 Cashflow improvement through cash collection

Figure 8.2 shows the difference between a collection rate of 57 DSO and 35 DSO and what it means in terms of cashflow and saved bank interest. A 22 day improvement or reduction in DSO from 57 days to 35 days improves the annual cashflow by £1 million. Bank interest of £135,000 can be saved in each succeeding year.

8.6 Guide to cash collection by telephone

INTRODUCTION

This is a general guide to cash collection by telephone. All the points mentioned in the guide could be brought up during one telephone call or over several calls.

Annual turnover (£ million)	Credit period (days)	Cost of credit 15% (bank interest) (%)	Amount of cash tied up by debtors (£)	Total cash (£)
15	57	351,000	2,342,000	2,693,000
15	35	216,000	1,438,000	1,654,000
Improvement	22	135,000	904,000	1,039,000

Improvement in cashflow in first year   £904,000

Savings in each succeeding year   £135,000

Figure 8.2 Cashflow improvement through cash collection.

There are only four reasons why customers do not pay in time:

(1) The customer cannot pay due to lack of funds.
(2) The customer deliberately sets out to pay late.
(3) Payment is held up due to inefficiency in administration – yours or the customer's.
(4) There is a query on the account.

AIM

The aim is to *persuade* customers to pay so that you can achieve your cash collection target.

REASON FOR PHONING

There are two main reasons why you will call customers.

Firstly, you will call to see if they have received the products and invoices your company dispatched to them. You may assume that these are in order. But it is more positive and shows a much more caring attitude towards the customers if you initially establish whether they are satisfied with the service they are getting. If you take this latter stance, you are adopting an *after-sales service* approach which is a friendlier way to do business. They may not have received your invoices.

It is important to time calls early in the process. For example, if you are collecting money for the period ended on 25 May it is a bit late to discover on 20 May that the customer has not got the invoice. This should have been discovered much earlier. The trick is to call as early as possible. For invoices dated, say, 12 April, you should check to see if these and the goods arrived and were acceptable by 22 April. You could do this checking while perhaps you are calling to confirm the April payment amount.

Purchase ledger people also have targets to achieve each month. Your check helps them to be clear about your account every month. In fact they may come to rely on you more and more. It is all good for business. If something is not correct and, say, the customer wants a credit note, you have got oceans of time to get it all sorted out before the payment becomes due.

The second main reason for phoning is to *request payment*. You would do this towards the end of the month and after you have assured yourself and the customer that all the invoices are valid and correct and basically ready for payment.

There may be other reasons you would phone customers. These might include answering queries, correcting mistakes or even thanking them when they have gone to a lot of trouble to help you. You would also call new customers to ask them how their system works.

When calling a *new customer* for the first time you should try to familiarize yourself with the way they do things. This will help you to fit in more easily with their programmes. If they hold staff meetings on Tuesday mornings you will know that is not the time to call.

On a new account you should find out how they treat your paperwork. How do they treat your goods dispatch notes, invoices, statements and credit notes? Who else deals with the paperwork in their organizations other than purchase ledger? Is the paperwork dealt with as it comes in and cleared on a regular time scale, or are there several times in the month when the various processes take place? There are many different ways of dealing with paperwork. Who authorizes payments? How and when does the computer system prepare cheques? Are payments sent by first class post?

With a new account you are interested in any comments, complimentary or otherwise, that are passed on services or goods supplied. Your company's performance relies on customer feedback. From your own point of view you can always bring up unusual comments or problems you can't solve at the next department meeting.

Cash collection is about asking questions and asking for information, and does not require you to do any demanding.

At the new account stage you should, after asking all the relevant questions and having taken into account whether the replies fit in with your company's way of doing things, mention your *terms of payment*. It is important that the customers know when you expect them to pay. After all you are prepared to go to any length to help them. They may be able to include your terms of payment in their systems so that payment automatically reaches you in time.

PAYMENT REQUEST PROBLEMS

Having earlier in the process confirmed that everything is in order *you call again* to confirm the amount that is to be paid and the date by which it is to be paid. When you are fairly certain that the payment will be what you expect, this call could be made about ten days to a week before payment is due. Some customers have a habit of just saying yes to anything you ask, but not delivering in the end. So it is worth checking the amount you are to be paid. If this amount differs from the amount you expect, then check off all the individual invoices with the customer. If you don't do this now (before payment date) you will have to do so when the account is overdue. So, if you will probably take the same amount of time to check these invoices some time in the future, you might just as well do so when you stand the chance of getting paid in time.

Should the customer have difficulty locating the particular invoices in question then you can arrange to call back at an appointed time, e.g. 12.30 p.m. on Thursday. When you make such an appointment, keep it. Always make a point of calling back on the dot. Customers note this.

When you are not sure about the customer's promise on the second call, because perhaps a new customer's employee does not know the ropes, do not be shy about calling again. This third phone call might be made with four days to go before due payment date. It would obviously be short, a quick confirmation. If you are afraid of maybe embarrassing the customer by this third ring you can always use another pretext as an excuse to make contact.

QUERIES

Where there is a problem due to a query this must be solved as soon as possible after the conversation. Chapter 10 deals exclusively with queries and how they should be solved. The customer must be left in no doubt that you are going to deal with the query. You should automatically apologize if your company is at fault. It does not matter whether you spend all day apologizing, or whether it is your fault. You are representing your company at that moment and that is how the customer sees it. In fact, if appropriate, you could always thank the customer for bringing the query to your attention (see Excuses below).

PAYMENT TERMS PROBLEM

If a customer will not meet your payment terms, you are basically in a negotiating position.

You have delivered your side of the contract by delivering the goods or supplying the service. You have presented your invoice which shows your payment terms. You need not be afraid to ask that these terms be met. But there are a few things to take into account before you press further:

- Has anyone in your organization agreed to alter the terms in this particular case?

- Is the customer operating an A, B, C stream method of paying suppliers? Some companies pay accounts according to numerous terms of payment, set out by them, rather than meet their suppliers' terms. These may be companies who feel that they are large enough to squeeze the finances of smaller or more vulnerable suppliers. Or they could be crisis driven companies that feel they have no other choice but to pay late. The A, B, C streams refer to how they treat individual suppliers.

  The A stream suppliers are the ones the companies do not want to upset since any disruption in supply would injure them. They must pay these suppliers on time. The B stream suppliers can sometimes be played off against one another if they do not like being paid late. The C stream suppliers are ones that they can either do without, or who cannot threaten them or who are small vulnerable outfits. Some companies put all new suppliers into the C stream and wait to see if they complain. They may on a vigorous complaint move the supplier into the B stream and wait again. This is, of course, not good business.

- Has someone in the customer's accounts office decided suddenly to pay your account late deliberately?

For reasons I have outlined in other parts of this book, it is not, all things being equal, good company policy to allow extended credit. However, it does happen and there are sometimes advantages to be gained.

If you are dealing with A, B, C streams or deliberate slow

payers you must talk the position through with your sales team, and anyone else who can contribute to your next appraoch to the slow payer. This is because when you go back to the customer you know you have your company's support. You must be clear in what you indicate to the customer. You have several options:

(1) The softer of these is to appeal to the customer's sense of fair play. Emphasize that your tight monthly commitment to management (or bank manager) relies on payments hitting your bank balance by certain dates each month, and please could the customer oblige you? Your company is holding down prices but with high interest and late payers you will not be able to peg back the prices for much longer (this must be true). Receiving a cheque in the current month clears the statement (or wins cash discount). You can even come up with the one about keeping customers efficient by keeping their finances current (this is true). There are other appealing gestures. Use them.

(2) Accept the fact that the customer is always going to be late and accept lower profit margins through higher bank interest charges.

(3) Increase prices for the particular customer to cover costs.

(4) Visit the customer. Talk to the buyer or the MD.

(5) At the next overall price increase add an amount to cover late payers.

(6) Do not include your usual discount for bulk buying.

(7) Refer the customer to your competitors.

A QUESTION OF THE AMOUNT

Amount disputed

The customer may sometimes challenge your account balance. There will, of course, be times when the balance the customer has on your account is different from the amount you are showing.

There are numerous reasons for this. Many systems are computerized. They are continually updated. Your system will show invoices that have been dispatched but which the customer has not yet received, while the customer's system will show payments that you have not yet received. There may be a credit note here, a debit note there. So you need to go through the entries to discover whether the customer has recorded all your charges.

You will first need to assure yourself that there is not a payment in the post or in the customer's system being sent to you. Here you have to be careful with the terminology. When the person speaking to you advises that the invoices are paid, he may be referring to the buyer's signature to pay. This may just be one of the processes en route to payment. And you need to know how the system works to anticipate when the payment will reach you. Then you need to mention:

- the oldest high-value invoices;
- other old charges (invoices, debit and credit notes and adjustments);
- more recent charges you feel the customer should also be showing;
- when you have gone through the list you show on your records, you then go through any other items showing on the customer's list.

If, after all this, you still cannot agree, you need to reconcile the disputed amounts with the customer. The sooner you do this the better. The problem will not go away. If you need help ask.

Unable to pay

You will on occasion encounter customers who are unable to meet their obligations to pay you the money the owe. These fall into three categories:

(1) Those who are short of funds over a short period.

(2) Those who are going to take a long time to recover.

(3) Those who will not recover and whose business will be wound up.

You need to establish quickly into which of these categories the particular customer falls, since this will have a bearing on the way you should react.

Normally you will have so many accounts to deal with that decisions may be taken in haste without looking at the long-term business relationships with individual customers. You will have to find another customer for every one that you lose. There are other long-term effects also. If you are too hard on the temporary embarrassments of perfectly healthy companies you may just be handing these customers to the competition on a plate. The effects of this on your company may be fatal.

You may not always have the last say yourself. But you can contribute to the decision. So you need to give the problem your best attention each time. After all if you are not credit manager now, you may want to be credit manager in the future. In that case you could start by thinking like one. So what do you have to consider?

What could have contributed to the customer's current problem?

- Perhaps the customer has ordered too much stock over a few months and is now having some difficulty moving the stock within the time planned. This may have been due partly to your own salespeople's efforts. And in fact if you had not sold the stock to the customer you might now be in the same position yourselves.

- It is possible that the market in general is currently slow but will pick up in a month or two.

- Perhaps a large order was lost at the last minute and stocks are temporarily high.

- One of the customer's normally fast-paying accounts did not pay on time but will pay next month. Could you advise them how to collect their accounts faster (in return for their paying you first in the future)? If they do have a problem collecting their debts could you advise them to take extra staff or temporary help, perhaps through the Institute of Credit Management (so that you can then treat the problem as short term)?

These are all problems that will disturb your collection target in the short term. It is a part of everyday life and can be annoying to you that you may miss your collection target. Try not to allow this to cloud your judgement on individual customers' payment records. It might calm your frustration to talk through the decisions you make with the salesperson responsible for the individual accounts.

In the short term you can allow the customer to pay late for one or two months. You may have no choice but to do so. It is frustrating. However, there is no universal requirement to show bad feeling towards the customer. All business is show business. Keep smiling, especially at the customer. You need the customer more than he needs you.

If the customer's problem is more long term, then the situation requires more penetrating questions asked of the customer. You may have to justify allowing further credit. You may even feel that stronger action is necessary to recover the debts.

How could the customer have got to the point where he has a long-term paying problem?

- The long-term problems could be more serious.
- A large competitor of the customer could have opened in the same street. The competitor could be offering reduced prices and this could have enticed business away. The customer may be taking stock of the situation with a view to staying open perhaps using a different sales strategy. For example, the customer could specialize in areas the large competitor has ignored or in which he is poorly represented. The small customer may ask you for more time to pay.
- The account could just have got behind in payments each month without being noticed. You may feel the customer will have to be brought more into line with your payment terms.

One method you could use to bring the accounts up to date is the gradual payoff plan.

The gradual payoff plan

The principle is shown in Table 8.1 where the customer is currently paying 30 days late. In this particular example the pay-

Table 8.1 Gradual payoff plan.

	Invoice period close Date	Payment received	Average DSO
Past	December 31	February 19	65
payments	January 31	March 20	63
	February 28	April 22	67
Gradual	March 31	May 21	66
phased	April 30	June 11	57
payments	May 31	July 3	48
	June 30	July 27	42
	July 31	August 20	35

ment terms are: 'Please pay by 20th of month following month of invoice'.

An advantage to agreeing to these terms, providing they are met, is that you don't then need to worry too much about this account.

Should the customer agree to a gradual payoff plan, you can look forward to the time when your cash collection target will be met.

If the customer does not agree then further consultation with senior management and the salesforce may be necessary. All the facts should be discussed before arriving at a decision.

This gives the company a chance to form a coordinated approach to a particular customer. In the long run, looking for the coordinated approach enables you to practise a sense of internal company cooperation and support. Where you are having trouble with an account you might normally talk with the sales rep. But when it reaches the stage of 'Will you or won't you stop supplies?' the sales manager ought to be given the information. The more you keep the channels open the more benefits will come your way. Try to get back to the customer as soon as possible to advise your decision.

If this decision means that you are to sue the customer, pass the case over to either a solicitor or a reputable debt collection agency. Then forget about it. You have other customers to worry about.

Cash collection is about communicating with a smile. A sense of proportion is called for, since because you are at the end of the sales process you will see all the mistakes others make including, of course, your own. Frustration can for this reason become part of your everyday life. You have to live with it. Or you can take it to your superiors with a structured and logical interest element, for their advice.

EXCUSES

There must be thousands of excuses that are used each day to put off credit people. They fall into various categories, samples of which are listed below.

Where the excuse/reason for non-payment, e.g. being unable to find paperwork, does not involve an error by you or your company, you have to face the possibility that you are being put off.

However, there is an approach you can take that should see off the excuse the next time around, and for the future. The simple method is to give the excuse purveyor a lot more work to do each time. A few samples are provided below.

Beware the staged excuse that goes over the top.

I know a finance director in the music business, who was once faced by a customer who brought his five children into the office to add weight to his reason for non-payment of the account.

The luxurious office in London's West End saw the five neatly turned-out children and the financial director listen intently to the father's pleading. It was quite an emotional scene. All he was asking for was a little time to get his act together. He laid a very loosely contrived plan out for the financial director to review. But as the atmosphere was highly charged what was going through the financial director's mind was having to face these lovely children a few weeks after they were left to starve on the streets of London. He allowed extended credit.

When the customer had left the office, the financial director reflected that he had allowed the customer the extra time to pay against his better judgement. The more he thought about it the worse he felt. How could he fall for such a cheap emotional trick? Who else would trust anyone who uses his family as a business bargaining tool? And what if these children were not his customer's but were in fact all part of an elaborate fiddle?

The next day he faced his credit manager with the details. They decided to check out some of the nagging details. This was just as well. They discovered that the customer could not possibly survive and was in fact in the process of closing his business in order to start a new company in another industry.

The money was quietly recovered. I suppose the moral is be nice, generous and sympathetic, but business is business, even when it is show business.

Other excuses are:

- It's in the post.
- It has been passed and is now awaiting signature.
- We have a query on this.
- The buyer hasn't passed it yet.
- Just this moment got your invoice.
- We don't seem to have received your invoice, copy please.
- Sorry, could we have another invoice copy.
- The computer's down, can you call back.
- The boss is on holiday, can't get it signed.
- I'll ring you back.
- He's away.
- I haven't got around to it yet.
- It came in too late for this month's run.
- He's busy.
- She's on holiday and I can't find the invoice.
- The MD is holding back all the invoices.
- According to our payment terms it's not due yet.
- We have extended credit on this.
- We are waiting for your credit note.
- We only pay on statement, where's yours?

- The invoices are in next month's run.
- We are still awaiting the goods.
- We have not had the service yet.
- We have cashflow problems.
- We have to await payment from our customers first.
- We do not have the funds to pay until next week.
- Your goods were faulty, please collect them.
- We sent your product back.
- Your invoices went to the wrong address.
- We thought you were going to collect the cheque.
- We put it into your bank last week, haven't you got it yet?
- We'll cancel the cheque that has gone astray and replace it.
- The accounts are at our accountants.
- The VAT man is looking at the accounts.
- The accounts are at the bureau.
- The person who deals with your account is out.
- We are changing over our computer system.

There are some slow payers that you accept, but why? There are others who require a little understanding now and then. These excuses are largely given to credit people by customers' employees to block their legitimate request for payment, simply because in the main they think it is the easy way out at the time.

If customers were to understand that each time they forwarded some lame pathetic excuse they were to be put under heavy scrutiny, they might feel inclined to give better service.

And it won't do them any harm at all to reflect on the value of the service they give. Purchase ledger people, like most of us, like to have complimentary days. Happy credit people make this possible. Fobbing off credit people does not make them feel better about themselves. Giving useful advice makes them feel good. Feeling that they were instrumental in getting your payment to you allows them to sleep easier. So by questioning the initial lame excuse you can see how happy you make them.

It could go something like this.
'It's in the post.'

The questions

As we have not yet received it . . .

- What day was it posted?
- Was it posted in the morning or the afternoon?
- Do you normally post first class or second class?
- Do you post cheques first class or second class?
- So which class do you think this would have gone?
- How does your system work?

  - Do you personally put it in the envelope?
  - If not who does?
  - Who handles it after you?
  - Where does it go after that?
  - How long would it normally take the cheque to reach the post room from the time you have finished with it?

- How much was the cheque for?
- How many invoices did it pay?
- What invoices were paid?
- Can we check to see that you have our correct name and address?
- If it does not turn up in the next two days can we have a repeat cheque?
- If it turns up I will call you to let you know.
- While we're talking there are a few queries we have solved for you.
- Could we see where the following invoices are in your system? Considering what's happened I'd like to make sure they are properly in your system.
- Now is there anything we can do that we are failing currently to do that would help you to process our invoices for payment?
- Can you give me the name of the next person along the processing line, post room, etc., for a quick word? It would

be a pity if after all your work they did not get it right. Thank you.

If after further questions of others you feel it would help to contact the purchase ledger person again, do so.
Another example might be:
'It came in too late for this month's run.'

The questions

- How does your system work?
  - What's the latest date invoice that you accept for this month's run?
  - Have we addressed it properly?
  - Where does it go first after your post room?
  - How long does your post room hold on to mail?
  - Who does what to the invoice?
  - How long does each process take?
  - Do you know the names of the people so I can contact them directly and so help you with that part of the process?
  - Some of our later invoices got on this month's run; why do you think that happened?
  - Do you go by the date of the invoice or when you get it?
  - If someone in your company holds up some of our invoices which should have been paid can you pay later ones instead?
  - I'll go through to your buyer to ask her advice and get back to you with the reason why it did not get on this month's run. Thank you for your help
- Then you call the buyer, cheque signatory, etc., with questions that are designed to get the correct answers to parts missed by purchase ledger and also to impress that it is taking longer than you anticipate to get paid. (Remember if the invoice is still showing as not been paid it is still showing against the buyer's budget in the purchase ledger and buyers do not normally like this. So bring it to their attention.)
- You offer help to each person that you question. You want to make everything easier for them. You want to be seen as a helper not a moaner.
- Then explain to the purchase ledger contact what you have found out.

A ROUND TOIT

The last time we spoke on
the telephone, I remember you mentioned
that you were unable to spare the time to get
around to it. So please accept this Round
Toit with our compliments

O'Sullivans Wines, Highbury, London
Tel 071-000-0000

Keep this ROUND TOIT
SAFE

Figure 8.3 'A Round Toit'.

For those customers that are always putting things off with the famous 'I haven't been able to get around to it', send them 'A Round Toit' – see Figure 8.3 for a possible design. These can be manufactured in plastic, to be used as coffee stands. This would keep your company name in front of the customer.

Make every phone call count. Speak to someone who can help. This need not always be the top man. Take the following example.

> A new member of staff phoned a new account that was behind in the first payment. A lady who picked up the phone said she was the charlady cleaning the MD's desk. She took down a message about drawing the MD's attention to a particular invoice and a possible return phone call.
> Two days later a cheque arrived with a complimentary letter to the new staff member thanking her for being patient and understanding while talking to his mother.

The best times to make a telephone call are:

- 9.00–12.30 each morning. This is the time when people are brightest, when they can find the information and when they are more willing to help. After lunch, following a meal with perhaps a glass of wine, they may be a little slower, sleepier and thinking about going home.

- Friday afternoon. With a few hours to go home for a weekend people will promise you anything. You can then follow this up early in the following week.

- Budget times. When you know the dates your customers' budgets are agreed you know that they have the money to pay you. Sometimes at the end of their financial year they just want to 'give it away'. Government departments and local authorities' budgets and budget times are well published. Get there before the competition.

THE COMPETITION

- Inland Revenue
- VAT
- Gas company
- Electricity company
- Local authorities
- Water company
- Other suppliers
    - A stream suppliers
    - B stream suppliers
    - YOU

YOUR EDGE

- Providing a first class service at all times, as described in this book.
- Other aids
    - Christmas cards
    - Birthday cards
    - Thank you cards
    - Flowers
    - Company product

- A visit around your factory
- A sit in on your staff session

When someone you meet remembers a Christmas card you sent to him eight years earlier doesn't that say volumes for the little effort you put in and the power of recall?

HOW MANY PHONE CALLS CAN A PERSON MAKE?

A question often asked is how many calls someone can make per day. This is a tough one. It depends on so many variables, plus what assumptions are made and the climate in which the operation is carried out.

The trouble is that picking a number that is too high for a particular operation would not be fair to the credit people. On the other hand, picking a number that is too low would be letting the questioner down. There are a number of aspects to consider.

Industry

If it is a traditional industry like farming, or a high-tech new industry like computers, the way things are done will affect the way a phone call will be made. For one thing farming is seasonal. Farmers may not stay in their offices to answer the phone.

What clout have you got in the industry? Can they do without your product? Does the average DSO in your industry give you enough time to be able to get around to calling all your customers?

Company culture

What is the attitude of your company to customers, the company departments and the individual member of the workforce? How does the company monitor performance and are the comparisons made against competitors or solely internal? Is the emphasis on market led or finance led management? Are individuals rewarded for their achievements? Is there team spirit?

A market led, performance monitoring, management style

will be more supportive of credit management than a finance led, autocratic style.

Internal communications

The geographical spread of internal communications may affect contact points. How well integrated are the company departments? Do production know what customers are saying about their products and do HQ people ever visit the far-flung branches? Do departments help each other or fight their corners? Are the company systems good, adequate or poor? A well-integrated company enables credit people to get their queries answered faster.

Credit department

What responsibilities does it have for order processing, billing, cashiering, accounts receivable (reconciling the accounts) and cash collection? Is the credit department split up into numerous specialist areas or is it integrated? When are accounts called? What support is there for the individual credit person? The more specialists you have the less effective you are.

Accounts

How many accounts are there to handle and what degree of difficulty is there, considering the other aspects mentioned above? Are they UK or overseas customers? How many accounts are the responsibility of the individual staff member and can they be adequately expected to manage that number? It is no good moaning at a staff member who is expected to collect money according to payment terms if he is trying to manage 6000 accounts in the fast-moving consumer goods sector.

Document flow

How many and what variety of documents does the individual deal with? What is the degree of complexity? How many items are on each invoice? Is the flow of documentation regular or do documents come in slow and fast streams? What kinds of queries have to be answered or passed on to be answered by someone else?

The individual

What experience does the individual have in business/credit? What skills do they have: communicative, numerative, commercial appreciation? Are they motivated? Are they being closely monitored? Are they given any training, internal or external?

The quality of the call

An after-sales service call will take longer than a quick third call for cash. But how much longer? Answering a query may be more complex than just confirming a pick-up time for a cheque. So how do you judge how long each call will take? Then there are times customers call you.

There is no substitute for actually making the calls and analysing the results. What you have to remember is to cover a period of at least one month to make it mean anything.

If you follow the recommended methods there will be four types of call to customers. You have to keep in mind that alongside the work involved in preparing the calls (such as getting the account details up on screen or even turning over the debtors' aged listing page) credit people will have constantly to communicate with other internal departments. This is to ignore for the moment other work they do as part of their routine.

Each of these calls would be expected to have a different intensity of conversation. The after-sales service call is the monthly or bimonthly call to check on any problem and to confirm receipt of goods, services and paperwork. This call may result in a lot of other work as the credit person corrects mistakes, passes on messages, or clears up misunderstandings. However, the second call in the month to the same customer will be less involved. And if you are able to make a third call, this should be very brief. Answering a query may take away time that could be spent on the phone talking to customers. But queries must be solved. Problems will not go away.

The quality of each call is more important than the number of calls. Quality will always win over quantity. There is sometimes a tendency to concentrate on the number of calls rather than the results of the exercise. At the same time calls *must* be made.

HOW TO ORGANIZE THE CALLS

You could decide that each time your people make a call they include in their conversation a mention of all outstanding invoices to keep the account in a sort of long-term current position. Towards the end of the current month they would also, of course, advise the customer of the amount you expect to receive in that month. The reasoning might be that in the long run you will reap the benefits from continually mentioning to the customers the amounts they owe like a continuing statement of account.

You might take the view that you are not going to be able to give the customers monthly attention because you do not have the staff to go around. Therefore, you call them every second month, unless their accounts become overdue for payment.

You might decide to call all high-value customers each month, and fit in the lower-valued ones who were overdue with calls every second month or as and when. You might hope that the latter cycle would encourage the lower-valued accounts to pay.

Having worked out your call strategy you may decide that you can't meet the targets set (hopefully you did not have a hand in setting them yourself). In this case you require more staff or more experienced staff. You may have to take staff away from particular specialist work and put them on to cash collection. You could also consider training. Hopefully your company can look at long-term improvements.

Many companies split up the credit department between numerate and communicative people. In fact they are sometimes hired to perform one or the other function. Where this is the case it is worth considering pairing a cash collector with a cash allocator. This would keep one in touch with the work of the other, and encourage team spirit. Otherwise you might create a 'them and us' in the credit department.

Whichever way you go, there is a need to quantify the reason, if only so that you understand why you are working in your particular way.

If you are working in the ways described in this and other chapters you are in a position to monitor the monthly credit management programme in detail. You will be able to tell:

- how long the average call takes, and you will be able to break down this detail into the type of call and the quality of the conversation, and of course the result;
- the degree of difficulty you are encountering in both cash collection and cash allocation;
- your query load (see Chapter 10).

From the analysis you may be left with a number of alternatives. You may try several until you hit the optimum. This could amount to making all the types of calls described above, each day by each credit person. Time could be put aside to reconcile a number of accounts each month. You could then plan the rest of the month around cash collection.

It is important to involve all credit department personnel in any programme both to get their ideas included and to gain their acceptance, which of course will be vital.

8.7 Cash collection by visiting the customer

Meeting people at their workplace to talk to them about their business has just got to be interesting. How they do things and why, especially when you have not seen things done their way before, must add value to your knowledge.

All meetings with customers must be well prepared. You must have a plan and know what you want to achieve. This should be more than or different from what you can achieve by simply talking on the telephone. See if you can get to see their operations, or if they are a manufacturer, their workfloor.

Make file notes of what you see. It is a learning process.

8.8 Cash collection by letter

Experience shows that a letter has a 33% chance of success. Say you have 4000 accounts and you dispatch 1500 letters. You will on average receive payments from 500 of these customers. The second letter will bring in 333. You are left with a further 667 customers still overdue and without queries on their accounts. Whatever the value of the accounts (and the value in terms of money is important) it is one-sixth of all the accounts. You could keep sending letters or hand the accounts to a debt collection agency for collection. It is not a very good record.

If the value of these 667 accounts is low, due perhaps to one order of say £50 outstanding on each account, then you could call into question the value to the company of allowing credit for such sums. Maybe there is another way of dealing with them.

But if the amounts are significant then the overall way that you deal with them must change. They should be included in the after-sales service calls stage of contact. If you can achieve this there will be no need to send them the normal overdue letter, since you will know why they are not paying.

Letters in themselves may cause more work for you than actually talking to the customers on the phone. Also in many cases they can be more expensive. For this reason they are really a last resort.

How you word a letter may depend on your line of business. If you were sending out a reminder for a company in the music business you might not, for instance, quote the invoice numbers. This might be because your system might not be able to cope or there might be so many. In that case it might be better for your letter to ask the customer to contact you to discuss the account. But, on the other hand, if you could supply all the outstanding invoice numbers and other details you would be giving the customers all the information they would need to respond.

You will not want to go over the top in a letter. However, you do need to spell out the situation to the customers. Give them every chance to respond. Advise them what you expect them to do. Also advise them what action you will take if they fail to respond.

Some companies send out up to four cash collection letters in their overdue payment cycle. This prolongs the agony. If the customers are not paying you and have not contacted you to explain why, they are either inefficient (and perhaps heading for broke) or playing unfair (holding on to their money for as long as possible at your expense). You owe it to yourself to get to the

```
                                  (Account No.               )

                                  Date


Dear

Re: Amount Overdue £

We are surprised that the above amount remains overdue for
payment.

Our terms of payment are stated on each invoice and
statement and are

        'Please pay within 30 days of invoice date.'

Should you encounter any difficulty in meeting these terms
of payment, or have any query on the invoices that we have
not yet answered to your satisfaction, or if you cannot
identify the amount to which we refer, would you please
contact the undersigned immediately.

If we do not receive payment of the amount shown above or
you do not respond positively to us within the next 5 days
we will suspend deliveries of product automatically.

We hope this action will not be necessary.

Yours sincerely




CREDIT DEPARTMENT
```

Figure 8.4 Sample letter 1.

```
                                   (Account No.              )

                                   Date

Dear

OVERDUE ACCOUNT — LEGAL ACTION

As we have not had any response from you following our
previous reminders for payment, we have suspended
deliveries of product.

We now find it necessary to enclose, for immediate
payment, the current and up-to-date statement of account
showing the balance due to us from you.

We must further advise that, unless the balance of the
account is fully paid by 10 o'clock on ...........of
...........199X, we will be left with no alternative but
to refer the account, plus costs, to other hands for
collection, without any further reference to you.

Yours sincerely




CREDIT MANAGER
```

Figure 8.5 Sample letter 2.

heart of the matter quickly. Besides you have other customers to service. Don't let them suffer. Figures 8.4 and 8.5 show two sample letters.

When the letters appear on your cash collection cycle is important. As mentioned above there is no need to wait until the customer can't remember your company name. The schedule in Figure 8.6 might be a typical cash collection cycle.

Delivery date/Invoice dispatched	Day 1
Customer after-sales service	Day 7
Second customer after-sales call	Day 8-14
Third call – cash collection	4-10 days prior to due date
Statement	Last day of month First day of new month
First letter	7 days overdue
Second letter	14 days overdue
Debt Collectors	21 days overdue

Figure 8.6 Typical cash collection cycle.

8.9 Summary

- A cash collection programme must be totally committed to action. It cannot afford to be handicapped by reams of procedures and cluttered by webs of indecision.

- The management structure, the systems, the routines, the training and the individuals must be geared to clearing the decks each month by being up to the minute in workflow.

- Good planning is essential. Forecasts will loom more important than history. Lessons learned must be fed back into the routine and training.

- Good communication skills are vital to seek cooperation from customers and internal departments alike. The time scale between order, invoice and payment should be used as a bench mark of how customers react to the company.

- Credit people are as much in the firing line as anyone in the company. They live in a sense in the customers' pockets, where customers keep their money.

- Two of the most common reasons why companies get over-stretched are poor management and losing a grip on their finances. Credit people try hard to remind them of their operating financial obligations. This in turn should keep them in touch with their current finances and hopefully give them a sense of reality. There is always the possibility that this may encourage slack customers to adopt better management practices.

- Cash collection essentially looks after the customers and their money.

Cash Allocation

Cash allocation is a thankless task that should be given more recognition.

Transferring data in the context of financial numbers is basic to any business. Skills are needed to allocate cash, interpret an array of sometimes conflicting messages from customers, internal management, procedures, training and documentation.

Very little constructive monitoring is currently evident. An attitude of 'just get on with it' prevails. Yet the tasks of the cash allocator are as central to business as any others. The transactions, which include understanding elements of the UK institutions of banking and accountancy as well as dealing direct with the market (customers) while working to their own company procedures, are as diverse as any in commerce.

There are about 250 different main UK accounting packages available. Accepting that some of these may be similar, many have very distinctive features that when appearing in the form of, say, remittance advices present varying profiles of difficulty to the cash allocator.

The whole routine is taken up by assessing and implementing very detailed information. Business succeeds by getting details right. Without a clear monitoring policy you cannot tell if the cash allocators are getting it right. If they fail on details, so does the company.

Their work must be monitored to retain the quality service. The process is simply to transfer data from customers' payment advice slips on to the customers' accounts. The advices will be paying items that have been charged to the customers and appear on their statements. These statements are presented to the customers normally 12 times a year. Simple enough! Sometimes customers may ignore the statements and just pay invoiced items as they receive them. Matching payments to invoices should not create a problem. However, lurking among the invoices are company credit notes and customer debit notes that do not quite match. There are odd adjustments on the account to which no one can attach a document. And there are the personnel changes.

How the personnel changes are made and what happens to their work is sometimes overlooked. But it should not be. Normally if the new person has cash allocation experience he will be left to his own devices. This is a fatalistic way to impress new staff. The reasoning behind this managerial judgement might appear to be complimentary to the individual concerned in that allowing him 'to get on with it' instils confidence in his ability to operate a new system, without apparent supervision. But it may also be seen, especially by the new member of the team, as isolation. On a more general note it demonstrates a lack of a coherent training policy.

The new person will continue to reconcile accounts in the way he has learned, irrespective of whether this is correct. If this happens in your company, your system may call for a different method of allocating cash. Or your department might not be able to understand how the new person reconciles accounts. Until he learns how his new company operates, he may continue the way he has worked for some time.

He may never appreciate the best way to complete the work routine. Yet how often is the last holder of the job blamed for the things that have seemingly gone wrong? And if he has been doing something wrong it may take ages to find out. He may not be to blame of course. Personnel have to be managed, especially new personnel. People would like to know if they are doing something wrong sooner rather than later. Take the following example.

I have a friend who is a keen swimmer. For months at a time he would swim an hour to an hour and a half a day.

On holiday he would increase the time spent swimming to between two and four hours. He just loved swimming. Every session was started with six lengths of butterfly. Sometimes when swimming in the local pool he noticed a swimmer passing him while he was doing the breast stroke. In local swimming pools there are, I am told, unofficial races where people try to pretend they are not racing until they pass the guy in front. On these occasions when he was passed, my friend would revert to the butterfly to catch up.

He had been swimming like this for 15 years before he discovered he had not being doing the butterfly in the right way.

He felt highly embarrassed about it. Throughout all these years no one, including one of his friends who was for a time in the US Olympic team short list, ever said anything to him.

Still at least he found out. In his case he wasn't making a fool out of anyone else. Not even his friends minded which way he swam.

However, read the following scenario.

Peter Ellis the new boy, has taken over from Sandie Peabody. Each reconciles the accounts in the way they learned before joining the company. Each reconciles accounts in a different way from the other. They have not been introduced to the company's integrated system (maybe because there isn't one). No one monitors what each has done and each has continually performed one task in the wrong way.

Now consider their customers experiencing similar problems in their purchase ledger departments. Because the staff in your company and the customers' staff do not recognize that they are doing wrong, this perhaps minor error may spread throughout the industry. You may find other examples of this sort of detail being missed in other areas of your organization. The most usual misunderstanding in other departments on accounting terms is the difference between a debit and a credit.

Think about the effect on the individual, say after 15 years of shuffling paper and figures around in an endless, partially senseless way and then suddenly discovering that he has been doing something basically wrong. All those company moves. If someone had just hinted at it way back. It would most assuredly have saved much effort.

The way to overcome such unease and waste of talent and skills is to introduce a monitoring system to catch the errors early.

Like everything else in business it is the details that count.

Technology will not mean much if you pass up the chance to get the detail right.

Senior managers are also quite capable of getting things wrong for 15 years. The business climate is sometimes not sharp enough to catch all the fallout from bad management practices in time. Here is an example of how management procedures get in the way of business.

I know of a credit manager working for a multinational pharmaceutical company who was asked to do the impossible.

His instructions arrived by memo. He was required to have *all* 2000 UK and overseas customer accounts reconciled with customers every 90 days. He had to send each customer a letter which had been prepared for him, showing the account balance at the end of the month and requesting the customers to reply in writing within 15 days. If the customer failed to reply he had to send a second letter and possibly a third letter. There was no provision for follow-up after that.

If the customers agreed the balances on their accounts their confirmation had to be countersigned by the financial controller. In addition, each month, the financial director required a report on progress.

The credit manager had joined the company two years previously. He had hired three staff who did not have cash collection or cash allocation experience. There had been a recent change of computer system and the staff had worked a lot of overtime to achieve the changeover. However, the brought-forward balance system was still with them. The cash collection record was well ahead of company expectations.

The main reconciliation problems were due to a confusing cash settlement discount message the company was giving customers. On the one hand, customers who paid outside the cash settlement discount terms were asked to repay the discount. And on the other hand, the company was reluctant to enforce the message. This state of affairs had gone on for a number of years. The credit manager had got involved in trying to reduce the amounts outstanding and disputed on cash settlement discount. But it was proving difficult without support. Then came the new instructions.

The potential damage the new instructions would have on the cash collection effort and general customer contact relationship was not lost on the credit manager. The collection position was awkward enough because of the confusing discount problem. But the manager thought that the intended recon- ciliation checks would seem like harassment to customers. In any case where there were differences, these were in the main due to discounts. It seemed like the continuation of a vicious circle.

The credit manager tried to limit the damage by initially sending out 100 letters to carefully chosen customers. There were 20 replies in the first 15 days. These were from customers whose accounts were temporarily showing credit balances. A second letter was dispatched to the other 80 customers. The few replies that were received were from customers who disputed the balances. By the time the third letter was ready to go out a second statement had been dispatched. This would then mean that the third letter would refer to a statement which was showing a different balance to the current statement.

The credit manager went back to the financial controller. He briefly explained the difficulties: more work for his staff, alienation of customers and that now that the programme was operating it could be seen that the work itself was becoming pointless. A date was arranged for a further meeting.

However, this meeting was overtaken by events. Two staff members resigned. The programme was abandonded. In the following three months both the financial director and the finan- cial controller were transferred to other divisions, in the normal course of their duty. Finally, the credit manager also resigned.

On the whole, employees who deal direct with customers relate more easily to customers than to figures. They understand that they can't treat customers like naughty children who get their sums wrong. The programme was not thought through. It broke team spirit. There was no consultation with the people that were to operate it. It marred the company's relationship with its customers. It did not anticipate customers' reactions. In fact it did not anticipate anyone's reaction.

The credit manager was put in the impossible position of asking his team to accept a programme of work that he and they knew to be flawed.

Sir John Harvey-Jones in his book *Making it Happen* puts it this way – 'An interesting fact about large industrial orga- nisations is that there is always a nearly unanimous clarity amongst those involved in the lower levels on who is actually keeping the thing going, because in every organisation some-body is.'

9.1 Plan the month

Planning the month prepares the way for easier administration.

The number of cheques can be anticipated. The degree of difficulty will depend on the number of current invoices, plus previous outstanding ones, accounts with balances, the DSO forecast and the cash collection record. A query element should be built in.

Over, say, a period of a few months, tight monitoring of cash allocation can produce time scales for allocating all types of accounts. Without this sort of information it would be difficult to know what human resources are needed to achieve success in any workplan. Most monitoring would have to be completed by staff members. This means that they would have to accept and operate the system. So it must be realistic and easy to understand. In order for them to accept any plan, they would automatically have to be involved with formulating it.

Although you may possibly get it right first time, you may not. However, since you have consulted everyone and continue to do so, a change should be easy to make. Some plans may start off in a general direction and be streamlined at a later date. In fact, you may discover that the exercise throws up points that you would never normally come across.

An alternative to planning is for everyone in the company to turn up on Monday morning (which in itself involves some planning) and to scratch around for something to do. There are some companies organized so informally that you may be left with the impression that everyone is doing his own thing.

But with an accurate and well talked through plan, wholly accepted by the workforce, you start from a positive position to attain a common aim.

9.2 Communication

Communication can be frustrating for cash allocators.

Most of their communication will be attempted at the stage where they are entering the details of payment on to customers' accounts. If we assume that in the normal course of events, most people, including customers' purchase ledger personnel, take holidays, go off sick, or are busy on the telephone, then the chances of always finding the contact at the right moment are slim. Some payment advices may cover hundreds of invoices and include numerous deductions. The cash allocator has to work out the best way to deal with each situation until he can reach his contact. This could happen several times a day. Each day may somehow appear incomplete.

Cash allocators need to confirm details with the cash collector. They will talk to sales, manufacturing and other departments about credits to be issued. Their entries on to the accounts affect the whole business. If they get it wrong, the mistake may be difficult to detect.

Merely to get anyone to listen to someone whose job primarily involves the simple transfer of data is in itself difficult. They need support.

9.3 Statements

It is unfair to expect customers and cash allocators to be given brought-forward statements. This is because the alternative, the open-item statement, is so much easier to follow.

Most computer changeover systems involve a change in brought-forward statements to open-item statements. There are normally two ways the changeover is completed.

The first of these is to reconcile each item on the old system, transfer these to the new system and add any current month's items. This takes very careful planning and involves a lot more work over a shorter time scale than the second way.

The second is to transfer the balance on each account over to the new system, along with current items. Over time the old balance will be reduced as the items are paid. In month two under the new system a start should be made to identify the unpaid balance items. Customers' attention should be drawn to these items.

Cash allocators are changing the profile of the sales accounts all day, each day, for paying customers. They ought to be given the best possible tools to do the job.

9.4 Possible routine

- Each day
  - collect mail 8.30 a.m.;
  - open mail and distribute;
  - separate and list cheques;
  - put account numbers against each payment slip;
  - distribute payment advices to cash allocators;
  - send cheque list and cheques to bank;
  - allocate cash to customers' accounts;
  - repeat above exercise for second post;
  - tackle queries:
      cash collectors,
      customers,
      other departments;
  - reconcile accounts, according to monthly plan;
  - input invoices (if part of work).

- Each week
  - check payments against bank statement;
  - review queries;
  - review reminder letter cycle.

- Each month
  - produce customer statements, and mail them;
  - discuss plan for coming month;
  - staff monthly meeting – credit department.

- Each year
  - annual personnel appraisal;

– year end accounts – contribution;
– holidays.

9.5 Summary

- The aim of the cash allocator should be to keep the customers' statements clean. That is to say clean of misunderstandings, clean of unwanted clutter, and clean so that customers concentrate on the important detail.
- Speed of turnaround is important. Cash should be allocated on the day it is received.
- The systems should be flexible. They must cater for all types of remittance advices and any combination of entering payments that will clear statements effectively. The recipient of the new statement should be given a clear understanding of what has happened and what is expected of him.
- Traditionally, the people rather than the systems have been blamed for errors. This is one area where it is imperative to 'go easy on the people but hard on the systems'.

Query Control/
Customer Feedback Information

Normally, 12% of company turnover is tied up in queries. This can be reduced to less than 1%.

There are various ways of tackling the problem. But the problem cannot be ignored. It will not go away, though the customers might.

There is too much at stake to try half-hearted measures. If customers feel ignored because their problems are not being solved quickly enough they will go elsewhere. If there is one thing worse than losing a customer, it is losing a customer to the competition. There is actually less work involved in actioning a query at the start of its life than having to face up to it eventually at a later date.

There is another reason for dealing with customer queries quickly. Over 90% of disappointed customers do not complain or return. Speed of response will encourage them to complain and stay. This even means on occasion that the error is corrected before the customer complains.

In a perverse way, correcting a mistake strengthens the business relationship. If everything goes like clockwork all the time it almost becomes automated and both supplier and customer lose the human touch which is basic to business. However, this does not mean that there is an obligation to make a deliberate mistake. It is just that having made the mistake, it is not the end of the world. An advantage can be gained by responding quickly to the initial error.

In the UK we plan for errors. Some of the competition does not. Take the following example.

There is the story about the UK car manufacturer who normally included a phrase in its contract to suppliers to the effect that it 'would only accept the consignment if there were no more than three faulty parts per thousand'.

A Japanese supplier won an initial contract to supply. When the first consignment was unloaded, the warehouse people found an extra package with a note. The note read 'This is first time we do business with UK. We do not understand instructions but we always try to please. So please find enclosed three faulty parts.'

A query control system can act as a pilot scheme before embarking on a full-blooded customer information system. It can also be used as a tool for change. It could revolutionize a company's internal operations, relationships with customers and overall market orientation stance.

10.1 Why have a system for queries?

(1) A query amounts to a misunderstanding with a customer. It slows down trading. It is criticism of the way a company operates.

(2) Failure to satisfy means that the customer will go to a competitor. It is easier and cheaper to satisfy a current customer than to find a new one.

(3) A query puts a human face on business. A supplier should be able to reaffirm in its answer, customer confidence in initial choice of supplier.

(4) A well-organized query system shows a caring attitude towards customers.

(5) The higher the quality of the service the more customers it attracts. Customers are prepared to pay more for a first-class service.

(6) A query system works like an audit on quality and adds a further dimension to quality control.

(7) Careful analysis of the queries will indicate general and specific customer concerns. This information, even used in its simplest application, can add to the marketing knowledge of the company and play a part in marketing strategy.

Having decided that a query control system might be a useful mechanism to have, it is then necessary to establish what kind of a problem there is.

10.2 Establish the facts

Find all the queries and record them. In the system demonstrated here the recording device is called a query log.

Record the type of query, e.g. faulty goods, invoice copy required. Record the amounts – the query amount and the invoice amount. The amount held up by the query might bear no relation to the size of the problem: e.g. the missing number plates and a £30,000 sportscar. Also, in some instances, customers will not pay any amount on their account because they want to draw attention to an unsolved problem.

Queries can be found everywhere. The usual places are in-trays, desk drawers, cabinets and customer files. They will be typed on customers' letterheading, scribbled on all kinds of odd bits of paper, telephone note pads, memo pads, computer paper, scrap pads. All of this suggests that there is no recognized way of treating customer comment. In this highlighted query control system the information is transferred to a query report, a format that can be recognized throughout the company as meaning action now!

Having established how many queries there are, their value and the amount they tie up in cashflow, the next step is how to deal with them.

10.3 Deal with the problems

A number of queries will need to be passed on to other departments for action; others can be actioned within the credit department. Brief details should be noted on customer files and high-value queries perhaps diarized for further follow-up. One way of following up is to check the query log every few days. In addition to the individuals' checking their own account query position, the credit manager should continually review the query log.

While recognizing that some queries may take more than a week to answer, generally the turnaround should take no more than a few days between receipt from customer and reply to customer. Some customer requests, such as copy invoice, should be actioned within minutes. Targets should be set to indicate what is expected.

The quality of the reply should be monitored closely. Half-hearted replies or amateurish efforts only expose the original mistake. The customer's confidence must be won back. Otherwise he will feel that he made a bad error of judgement in choosing the supplier. The answer is to return the compliment of being chosen by supplying a first-class quality service.

10.4 Strategic aims

There are a number of strategic management options available and gains to be made:

(1) There is the simply strategy of answering queries to:

    (a) satisfy customer needs;
    (b) reduce the DSO;
    (c) streamline administration.

(2) Some companies operate in an internally pressurized atmosphere without much regard to outside influences. Change is difficult. Customer comment may be the only way to refocus company attitudes on to the marketplace.

(3) The query control system is only a short simple step away from what could be a much larger and more detailed customer feedback information system. A more detailed system, although as simple to operate, could further expose

all other department personnel to the customer-orientated approach.

(4) The query control system focuses on the customers while involving continual contact between credit and other departments. This leads to a more integrated company. This integration, having being put on firm and neutral ground by the customer orientation element, is capable of expansion. Personnel and departments that do not normally contact each other could be linked. For example, they could get involved in special customer project-solving teams, as a result of the initial introduction via the query system.

Any of these programmes could in time be attached to the query control/customer feedback information system. It is worth getting it clear at the start. That way people can see where it and they are going.

10.5 What might be replaced

- A sales manager once picked up a telex which had lain hidden among his pending paperwork. It read 'Please supply 2000 coaches (buses) within the next six weeks'. An overseas name and address followed. It was dated the previous day. It was also absolutely genuine. Query control would replace many of the odd bits of paper.

- Uncoordinated departments fighting their corners do so at the expense of customer care. Some customers ring several departments to get action. There can be much duplication of work. A query system replaces this with a sense of order.

- Thinking dominated by internal company procedures and performance indicators, which may bear little relevance to the market, is badly focused. Bureaucratic practices and demeaning rules all come in for close investigation. Query control redirects thinking.

10.6 The short-term strategy

In the short term the aims might be:

- to deal quickly and effectively with customer queries;
- to encourage customers to make contact;
- to reduce the DSO.

10.7 The long-term strategy

The long-term aims might be:

- to expose all company departments to customers, so that they understand the customer's needs and fears and at all times put the customer first;
- to gear all company management reporting to customer- and market-related performances;
- to encourage customer information gathering throughout the company in order to help the marketing department and the board to formulate a more accurate market strategy.

10.8 Selling the concept

There are several advantages to be gained by both management and staff in accepting the system. Some of these advantages are exclusive to each.

MANAGEMENT

Management is informed by customers what is wrong with their products and services. Customers may even point to how to put the problems right. This is quality control at its most critical. An extended quality control practice, arising from the query control feedback, might be to encourage manufacturing personnel to visit customers. Perhaps they could form small project teams with customers. This would keep quality control under microscopic review and might even lead to joint new ideas with customers.

The involvement of any customer information system puts management in closer touch with the market. In the short term, management can act immediately on customers' concerns. Long-term analysis of information can lead to management's picking up on customer trends in purchasing before competitors catch on.

It can reverse negative skills in person-to-person internal management. Some managers shy away from confrontational issues especially with key personnel. This only avoids the imme-diate short-term problem. But the problem will not go away. When managers are seen not to manage, their department is the first to notice. The customer might be the next. Query con-trol offers a way out. The manager can indicate that it is the customers who are complaining about the service and not the manager. This way the confrontation is avoided.

Query control increases efficiency and reduces waste. Performances of individual workforce members as well as departments are monitored. Problems are pinpointed and are, therefore, more easily managed.

STAFF

Staff will see it as a fair system, since it is generated by cus-tomers. It will be seen as impartial.

Staff relate better to customers than to company financial accounts and reports. They will be able to appreciate the finer points. It is something to which they will feel more able to contribute. They will be able to make an impression which is recognizable.

When errors occur the query will generally be directed to the originator of the error. This will encourage the individual to learn from mistakes. It will also help the individual to solve problems. This, in turn, will help people to understand the business they are in.

Perhaps contrary to general belief, staff do like to have their work appreciated. They want to be monitored so that they can demonstrate how well they perform. Query control monitors their ability to get it right first time, and how to respond if they make an initial mistake.

It is also a way of spreading greater understanding of the company when staff are constantly required to contact other departments. It must be difficult in the normal course of events for a production workfloor worker to get a grip on the fears of a cash allocator. Even small isolated departments like R & D can become more integrated. Everybody makes mistakes, so all are brought into the system.

Personnel who operate in customer contact functions cannot always get their ideas or those of their customers to senior management. This may be because they feel their own manager does not always give their ideas enough thought. Their ideas normally coincide with those of the customers they serve. All customer comments can easily become part of the system and so, in effect, one small step away from personnel getting their own ideas aired. And, to coin a phrase, one giant leap for them. Since they deal with the work relating to query-solving each day they are the experts perhaps without being recognized as such.

The sooner they are recognized for the experts they are, the more they will contribute. On occasion the recognition comes late. Take this example.

There is the story about the retired oilman who was called back into the works in which he has spent 25 years as a fitter. He was asked to locate an air bubble which was blocking the oil supply.

He wanted to charge consultancy fees for the work. The works manager asked him to name his fee. He was desperate to get the oil flowing again.

The retired fitter, now consultant, took five minutes at the works to locate and get rid of the air bubble.

The works manager rang him following receipt of his charges, a bill for $2030.12. He expressed delight at the remarkable speed with which the work was carried out. He had no trouble with the fee charged. But he was curious about how the consultant arrived at the charge.

The answer was $30.00 for petrol, 12 cents for hire of the equipment (the hammer with which he tapped the pipes), and $2000.00 for knowing where the air bubble was.

10.9 The mechanism

The system presented here is an integrated query control/ customer feedback information programme. In its simplest form it consists of:

- a query report of customer query/comment;
- a query log to record and keep trace of the query reports; and
- a query summary of the monthly performance report.

Each individual in the credit department retains blank query reports. When one is completed it is logged in the query log and given a number. The manager reports on the monthly position via the query summary.

THE QUERY REPORT

The query report (Figure 10.1) sets out the customer details, the customer complaint/comment details, the elements of the query and the amount of the invoice. There is space for a reply.

Before being dispatched to the relevant department/individual it is given a log number. The query type is noted to enable the performance analysis monthly report (the query summary) to be completed.

A brief note is made in the customer file. Some computer systems allow space to make brief notes on the account.

To dispatch simply fold the query report, staple and address. There is no need to keep copies. On high value queries it might be a good idea to diarize when you expect to receive a reply.

The recipient will either reply to the customer direct or return the report to the credit department. The credit department then calls the customer. Where the recipient replies direct

QUERY REPORT (Customer Feedback) | Query No.

TO _____

DEPARTMENT _____ DATE _____

TEL _____

LOCATION _____

FROM   DEPARTMENT _____

CUSTOMER NAME _____

ADDRESS _____

Account
No.

PUBLICATION _____

TYPE _____

INSERTION DATES _____

QUERY DETAILS (or action to take)   QUERY
TYPE

	Invoice No.	Date	Amount

REPLY   FROM _____   DATE _____

QUERY TYPE KEY					
	AI	Address Incorrect	IC	Incorrect Category	ON Order Number
	CI	Copy Invoice	ID	Invoice Duplication	P Price
	DC	Discount, Commission	M	Miscellaneous	POP Proof of Publishing
	DNA	Did Not Appear	NO	Not Ordered	T Transfer

Figure 10.1 Query report.

to the customer he should send the report back to the credit department, with a brief note of action taken.

The question of lost query reports would be a problem for internal post or the recipient department. This would raise several other questions. The positive approach to take is to expect the mail always to reach its destination.

To summarize, it is only neccessary to use one piece of paper on each customer query.

Note The specimen report was designed for a newspaper company. The design should be kept as simple as possible.

THE QUERY LOG

The query log (Figure 10.2) lists the number and amount of queries for analysis and tracing reasons.

This can be located central to the credit department users. Each time someone completes a query report they record it on the log.

As each query is actioned the details are entered in the log and the query report either stored for future analysis or thrown away.

There are five useful interim trends that may show up on the query log before any formal analysis is completed:

(1) A type of query – incorrect pricing of a product.

(2) A particular customer – having what appears to be an unusual number of queries.

(3) A marked increase in the query value versus the invoice value.

(4) A sudden increase in the number of queries.

(5) A noted increase in the turnaround time on taking action.

Immediate action can be taken to solve what could otherwise become a major embarrassment.

In the normal course of events the log would be analysed each month and the picture of the company's performance shown on the query summary.

Note The specimen log was designed for a builder's merchant.

DATE	NO.	TYPE	INVOICE VALUE	QUERY VALUE	DATE REPLY REC'D	DATE ACT'D	CUSTOMER NO.	CUSTOMER NAME

QUERY TYPE KEY	D	Discount		IA	Incorrect Address
	DM	Damaged Materials		M	Miscellaneous
	FD	Faulty work Dry		NA	Not Authorized
	FF	Faulty work Floor		ON	Order Number
	FW	Faulty work Wet		P	Price
	IC	Invoice Copy		WN	Work Not Completed

Figure 10.2 Query log.

THE QUERY SUMMARY

The summary (Figure 10.3) analyses the position of customer queries, that is the trends in numbers of queries received, actioned and those remaining to be solved, and the trends in the particular type of query.

In selecting the cause or type of query whenever a choice has to be made between the number and the amount, it is the amount that must always be considered the most important. Selecting the causes to feature should become obvious as the first batch of queries is listed. In time the individual causes featured would be expected to change.

Experience shows that 12 is about the maximum number of categories that it is reasonable for users to hold in mind. Any more and they will begin to lose interest in the programme. *Note* the particular specimen example was designed for a high-tech office equipment distributor.

BOARD REPORT

Finally a space for the trend in customer queries is found on the directors' monthly report presented to the board (Figure 10.4). The sales outstanding aged analysis report indicates the number and invoice value of queries each month. In the forecast section of the report it also tries to anticipate the value of the queries. The forecast amount is translated into DSO for quick reference.

10.10 Summary

- Customers tend to feel better serviced by a company that quickly corrects its mistakes, than one that makes no mistakes.

- Credit management is at the end of the commercial process. It sees most of the mistakes that are made. It sees these mistakes through customers' reluctance to pay their accounts.

PERIOD	QUERY SUMMARY						CUSTOMER FEEDBACK REPORT	
	c/f last month		rec'd this mth		resolved this month		total to resolve	
CAUSE	NO.	VALUE	NO.	VALUE	NO.	VALUE	NO.	VALUE
Address Incorrect								
Price								
Discount								
Goods Damaged								
Copy Invoice								
Order Number								
Delay in Delivery								
Invoice Duplication								
Not Ordered								
Proof of Delivery								
Terms of Payment								
Miscellaneous								
TOTALS								

Figure 10.3 Query summary.

SALES OUTSTANDING AGED ANALYSIS REPORT   Period_____

Queries	
No	Amount

COMMENT

Query forecast	
Amount	DSO

Figure 10.4 Sales outstanding aged analysis report.

- A successful company needs to correct these mistakes at an early stage, and learn lessons. Otherwise the company will eventually fail to deliver. A method of recording, actioning and monitoring what happens in the short term is vital to company progress. One answer is actively to pursue an effective customer feedback information system described here.

- Measurement of performance should be put into context:
  - total value of queries measured in DSO (credit dept);
  - total number of queries measured against number of customers and invoices (sales transactions) (sales dept);
  - response time turnaround by individual departments (operations director);
  - improvements in quality of product and service (board).

  Some companies get their best ideas from customers. Staying more in touch with them helps mutual progress.

- A query system incorporates a large element of customer participation. This not only draws customer information, i.e. outside information, into a normal company reporting cycle, it also draws the company out into the marketplace, i.e. worrying how the market – customers – thinks.

- The marketplace is an ever changing world. Any system that relates to the marketplace reflects change. An effective query system contains an element of change. This is because change is automatically built into the system. Change is, therefore, more acceptable.

- Any customer information is an extra bonus to the marketing department. It also performs a quality control on other departments. All of this benefits the company.

Exports

Considering the UK current balance of payment problem, exporting is definitely a challenge. For the efficient credit management team it offers another chance to shine.

'Some considerations' (Figure 11.1) indicate the degree of involvement that faces the exporter and the credit manager.

Difficulties are compounded by lack of interest in and knowledge of other people's cultures, living standards and living styles.

Are we careful about mentioning hangovers to the Saudis? Do we send New Year cards to the Chinese on their New Year? Do we address Pakistani customers with their family name first?

Another difference might include a standard of living indicator. Using a forecast 1990 gross domestic product per head of population as a rough guide, and using US dollars as currency, the UK measures up to $16,300, the USA $22,200, Sweden $25,000, France $19,200, Japan $25,990, Norway $25,300, Nigeria $236, Brazil $2,264, India $350, Italy $17,300.

When talking to customers within the European Community it might help if we knew a little more about their day-to-day existence and what is important to them. For example, in terms of disposable income, the Danes spend most on housing – 20%. We in the UK, along with the Danes and Italians, spend most on leisure – 10%. The Portuguese and Irish spend most on food – 40%. The Germans and French spend most on clothes and the Belgians spend most on household goods and services.

Another indicator of lifestyle is where people live. In the UK the forecast for 1990 is that urban population will reach

The market

Exporters
Insurers
Freight forwarders
Shipping companies
Airlines
Chamber of commerce
Banks
Export finance houses
Confirming houses
Factors
Customs and Excise
Embassies
Overseas customers

Documents

Export invoice
Bill of lading
Air waybill
Certificate of insurance
Certificate of origin
Letters of credit
CMR note
CIM consignment note
Forwarder's certificate of receipt/transport
Standard shipping note
Dangerous goods note
Customs declarations
SAD
ATA + community carnets
EC free and preferential trade agreement documents
Export and import licences

Terms of transport

Ex-works (EXW)
Free carrier (FCA)
Free on board (FOB)
Cost and freight (CFR)
Cost insurance and freight (CIF)
Carriage paid (CPT)
Carriage and insurance paid (CIP)
Delivery duty unpaid (DDU)
Delivery duty paid (DDP)

Customers

Culture
Customs
Language
Politics
Religion
Race
Regulations
Time zones
Distance
Routes
Life styles
Standard of living
Currencies

Terms of Payment

Open account
Bill of exchange
Letter of credit

Figure 11.1 Exports: some considerations.

91%, while in Portugal it will be 31%. In the UK, the population spread is 233 people to the square kilometre, while in Ireland it is 50.

There are other differences. The UK is a financial led economy guided in the main by bankers, the City and accountants, who collectively seem to favour the short-term approach. On the other hand, the Japanese and Germans tend to be marketing orientated and take a long-term view on investment. In 1987 the biggest increase in small business in the UK was in the financial services field. By contrast, the Italians with the same size population as the UK have 60% of the working population self-employed across industries. The Italians' standard of living is higher than ours in the UK.

Where does this leave the credit manager? UK credit managers *must* satisfy themselves that the customer can and will pay. The more information they have the better they will do. The information can come from a variety of sources, both in the UK and overseas. The ability to get by without delivering is not an option for the credit manager. And although overseas bad debts do not get into the news very much, when they do it is worth noting which companies are involved. Banks could be expected to know more than most credit managers. Yet the kind of bad debt provision and bad debts currently seen in the big UK banks does not exactly inspire confidence in their ability to advise credit managers. However, banks are a source of information. The fact that they do not deliver their own operations according to plan does not necessarily invalidate their advice.

What it does indicate is that all information from whatever source needs to be cross-checked. Cross-checking picks up the general as well as the specific that can add to accurate decision making. Information sources have different perceptions on the same material. It is worth looking at all the angles.

Penalties are heavier for getting it wrong on the overseas market.

In 1992 we in the UK will be dealing more and more on open account payment terms. We expect our overseas customers to speak to us in English. Our important European trading partners have better trained and qualified managements and more skilled workforces. This puts our companies at a disadvantage. Collecting precise, accurate and useful information is the very least we can do to try and redress the balance.

From the credit management point of view, if the money is not collected, pointing out an inadequate company management position is not going to get anywhere. There is a real need to get in among the decision makers with accurate information on customers, the general market and the requirements both to compete and deliver.

11.1 Sources of information

INTRODUCTION

The key to getting it right is getting accurate information.

Any company wishing to collect information must be set up to do so. With most companies this does not require any big investment in finance or disruption to personnel. However, it does require some thought. There ought to be an awareness of where the information lies, how it is to be collected, how to evaluate it and how to use it.

In the following pages are listed a range of information sources and how they can help. There are most assuredly others. For instance, is the ultimate information source the customers, other exporters, reference books and literature, institutions in the UK and overseas, such as The Institute of British Management, The Institute of Directors, the CBI and the TUC?

CRONER'S REFERENCE BOOK FOR EXPORTERS

It is vital to keep up to date with the complex and changing world of exporting. One way to do this is to subscribe to *Croner's*.

This is a loose-leaf book which is updated monthly. It provides concise information on:

- how to export;
- import and exchange control regulations;
- documentation and consular information;
- packing and marking, etc.;
- requirements of overseas countries (see Figure 11.2);
- UK provisions and export control;
- customs procedures;
- export finance;

- insurance;

- postal information;

- VAT.

The cost of the annual subscription (1990) is £78.80 and currently £48.30 for annual renewal.

Additionally, all subscribers receive a monthly magazine which keeps them up to date on developments such as trade missions and business travel.

JANUARY, 1990   JAMAICA

Independent state within the Commonwealth situated in the Caribbean. Member of the Caribbean Common Market (CARICOM). **Capital:** Kingston. **Population:** 2.35 million. **Principal Ports:** Kingston and Montego Bay

LANGUAGE: English.

WEIGHTS AND MEASURES: British and Metric systems.

ELECTRICITY SUPPLY: Domestic: 110-220v. 50 cycles single phase.
Industrial: 220v. 3 phase.

CURRENCY: 1 Jamaica Dollar = 100 Cents.

EXCHANGE RATE: Jam. $10.10 = £1 Sterling

INTERNATIONAL DIRECT DIALLING CODES: Jamaica: 010 1809.

TIME: 5 hours behind GMT (6 hours behind BST).

PUBLIC HOLIDAYS: Jan 1; Ash Wednesday; Good Friday; Easter Monday; May 23, First Monday in August; Third Monday in October; Dec. 25, 26.

ENQUIRIES: Jamaican High Commission, 1 Prince Consort Road, London SW7 2BZ. (Tel: 01-823 9911); open 9.30-5.30, closed Sats.

BRITISH HIGH COMMISSION: PO Box 575, Trafalgar Road, Kingston 10 (Tel: 926 9050; Telex: 2110 a/b UKREP KINJA; Fax: 929 7869).

CHAMBERS OF COMMERCE: Incorporated Commonwealth Chambers of Commerce and Industry of the Caribbean, PO Box 499, Port of Spain, Trinidad; Jamaica Chamber of Commerce, PO Box 172, 7-8 East Parade, Kingston, Jamaica.

IMPORT RESTRICTIONS: Imports from South Africa are prohibited; Import licence required only for a limited amount of goods.

EXCHANGE CONTROL: Exchange control covers payments to all countries. Exchange Control approval required for advance payments in excess of US $2,000.00.

BILLS OF LADING: No special regulations. May be made out "to order".

CONSULAR INVOICES: None.

CERTIFICATES OF ORIGIN: None.

COMMERCIAL INVOICES: Must show the following particulars seller (name, full address, country), consignee (name, full address, country), port of loading, country of final destination, name of ship/flight no., other transport information, invoice date and number, customer's order number, other references, buyer (if other than consignee), presenting bank, country of origin of goods, terms and conditions of delivery and payment, currency of sale, marks and numbers, description of goods, gross and nett weights (kg), cube (m³) number and kind of packages, specification of

CRONER'S REFERENCE BOOK FOR EXPORTERS

Figure 11.2 Extract from *Croner's Reference Book for Exporters*.

Staff at Croner's are also willing to give advice.

BANKS

Banks produce leaflets giving general economic information on countries throughout the world. The leaflets can be picked up at the counter.

Banks will probably finance your exporting, either by overdrafts or by special arrangements. Such financial help depends on your delivering your side, i.e. products of good standard, on time and accompanied by correct paperwork. If there is any uncertainly on your side, the banks provide checklists to help get the details right.

Banks, however well intentioned their advertising blurb, rely on their branch managers to deliver operations. Managers can be very different in outlook, skills, flexibility and ability to understand your requirements. It isn't unknown for a manager to drive business away in droves.

It is important to recognize a difference in emphasis created by a new manager. It is reflected in the staff's attitude to your staff and paperwork. It also affects your customer's bank and ultimately your customer. It is essential, therefore, to know your bank manager (and his intentions for the branch).

Finding out how they do things and understanding the bank's methods, processes, terms and jargon enables a clear picture to emerge as to how the bank is able to help. If the customer's payment initially goes through the bank you'll want to know how long it is held before being transferred into your account. Any delay affects your cashflow and bank interest charges.

Exchange rates can be a headache, especially when the currency markets are fluctuating greatly. There is a choice available:

- Spot transactions
- Forward exchange contracts
- Foreign currency options
- European Currency Unit or ECU

The bank can insure against loss on exchange rates. The bank should advise on what is best for the individual case.

INSURANCE

Talking with insurance companies can reveal a wealth of useful information. Both insurance markets, covering loss or damage to goods and non-payment, rely on accurate assessment of the risks and, therefore, a knowledge of the market environment.

The combination of factors that could possibly go wrong makes insuring against loss or damage to goods an indispensable part of export costs. Lloyd's underwriters or the marine arm of your current insurance company are obvious routes to go for insuring goods.

Insuring against non-payment may also be an obvious decision to make. This, however, will depend on a number of factors: the general market; specific customers; the geographical area; the product lines; the terms of payment and the ability of the credit department. Many companies get by without taking out insurance against non-payment. Yet others may not be able to survive if just one of the invoices goes unpaid.

The major insurer in the UK covering non-payment is the Export Credit Guarantee Department (ECGD). ECGD offers the most comprehensive insurance:

- up to 95% of the invoice value
- specific markets insured
- comprehensive insurance world wide

If customers do not pay, ECGD will generally pay out at from one to six months after due payment date. Exporters are required to make credit checks on overseas customers. Declarations of sales are made each month to ECGD.

Their experience is world wide. They are a good source for risk information. If, for example, they refuse to insure a particular shipment it is probably not worth the risk.

FREIGHT FORWARDERS

Freight forwarders are in the business of supervising the movement of goods.

Anyone who has ever waited at ports, air or sea, or even railway stations or clogged roads, will appreciate the sort of problems that freight forwarders have to overcome. They advise on:

- the mode of transport
- the carriers to use
- documentation
- customs clearance
- packing
- insurance
- warehousing
- distribution

Because freight forwarders are engaged in handling the day-to-day transport of goods, they have up-to-the-minute information on the best route to go. This gives them an edge on all but the large company export/transport departments. The edge they have will be on safer routes, faster delivery times and costs. Freight forwarders are a source of information that is difficult to bypass.

EXPORT FINANCE HOUSES AND CONFIRMING HOUSES

Export finance houses offer two services to the exporter:

(1) They can act as the exporter's export department. They know the ropes. They understand the markets. Using an export finance house frees the administration efforts of the exporter. The exporter can then concentrate more on producing and marketing the products.

(2) They buy the goods direct from the exporter in the UK. This means that the exporter does not have to worry about

non-payment of invoices. The exporter is, therefore, able to plan cashflow more accurately.

Export finance houses can also introduce new customers to an exporter. They work on a network of overseas agents. This makes them a useful source of information to the exporter.

A confirming house acts as an agent to the overseas buyer. The goods are sold to the UK confirming house and this avoids the overseas non-payment risk.

Some export finance houses and confirming houses tend to specialize in a particular geographical area, or market segment. Exporters need to weigh up the advantages of dealing with an exporting house as against, say, bank overdraft or using their own exporting department.

DEPARTMENT OF TRADE AND INDUSTRY

The DTI can help with research, tariffs, regulations, licences and technical expertise. Many of the services are free and some, such as special market information research, are charged at very reasonable rates.

The Export Marketing Information Centre in London is open for desk research. It keeps a range of overseas statistics.

The DTI organizes overseas trade missions and is involved in trade fairs. These will be set up with help from UK overseas diplomats.

Broadly, the DTI gives a general or specific perception of the market and/or country or area in which exporters wish to operate. Since it is a government department its view will be detached from the other organizations mentioned here. This may be neither good nor bad news, just different. DTI spokespeople may for instance be voicing some notes from their opposite numbers in government departments in other countries.

From the credit department's viewpoint any information which may affect the collection of overseas debts is valuable. Although the institutional language may differ from source to source, this is perhaps in keeping with languages generally of the overseas customers.

SITPRO

SITPRO (The Simpler Trade Procedures Board) tries on one level to reduce red tape in country-to-country export/import procedures and on another produces documentation aids for exporters.

- SITPRO overlays involve typing a master document, which when checked will be used with a series of SITPRO overlays (plastic transparencies with the different form designs printed on the front) to create the individual forms needed for an export consignment.

    The system will produce documentation which meets international regulations. No special machinery is required other than a typewriter and basic photocopier (see Figure 11.3).
- Spex 3 is the computerized software package that does the same job, only much faster.

USEFUL ADDRESSES

Croner Publications Ltd, Croner House, London Road, Kingston upon Thames, Surrey KT2 6SR. Tel. 081 547 3333.

Up-to-date loose-leaf subscription service, monthly update covering most aspects of exporting. Monthly magazine.

Department of Trade and Industry, Export Market Information Centre, 1 Victoria Street, London SW1 0ET. Tel. 071 215 5445.

General and specific market advice. There are regional offices.

SITPRO, Venture House, 29 Glasshouse Street, London W1R 5RG. Tel. 071 287 3525.

Practical documentation completion help, both manual and computerized.

ECGD (Export Credit Guarantee Department), PO Box 272, 50 Ludgate Hill, London EC4AM 7AY. Tel. 071 382 7000.

Credit insurance against non-payment There are regional offices.

Figure 11.3 How to use SITPRO overlays.

Institute of Export, 64 Clifton Street, London EC2 4HB. Tel. 071 247 9812.

Aims to raise the standards of export practice, through training and exchange of ideas between exporters.

Association of British Chambers of Commerce, 212A Shaftesbury Avenue, London EC2H 8EW. Tel. 071 240 5831.

Advice. Local offices stamp certificates of origin.

British International Freight Association (BIFA), Redfern House, Boswells Lane, Feltham, Middlesex TW13 7EP. Tel. 081 844 2266.

Carries out transport arrangements for greater part of UK exporters.

British Exporters Association, 16 Dartmouth Street, London SW1H 9BL. Tel. 071 222 5419.

Members are fully conversent with all aspects of international trade.

11.2 Methods of payment

OPEN ACCOUNT

The goods and documents are sent direct to the overseas buyer who pays for them within a certain period. Generally there is no reason why normal UK terms cannot be negotiated. The tendency in some countries is to ask for more and more time to pay. The exporter's response need be no different than the response given to UK customers. What tends to happen is that UK exporters give overseas customers more time to pay just because they are overseas. This makes life more difficult for other UK exporters to negotiate reasonable terms of payment. For example, the French seem to understand that UK exporters will accept 90 day payment terms. The word simply gets around as to what is negotiable. Allowing 90 days' credit to customers in European Community countries is basically financing their operations.

Open account credit terms are the easiest way to do business. They are also the most risky. Gaining and using extensive knowledge of the customers and the market reduces the risk. It follows that open account terms are only offered to customers where the risks (as far as possible) are known to be within acceptable limits. In the UK you can jump into a car and visit the customer. This approach ought to be carried out in overseas trade too.

In this age of information technology there is no reason why knowledge of overseas customers in whatever geographical area cannot be brought up to the same level as UK customers. In the UK we possess the means. We just need to apply them.

The aim to build up a solid open account business is moving in the right direction to secure a wide customer base and rapid and regular payment structure.

BILLS OF EXCHANGE

The legal definition of a bill of exchange is 'an unconditional order in writing, addressed by one person to another, signed by the person giving it, requiring the person to whom it is addressed to pay on demand or at a fixed or determined future time, a certain sum in money, or to the order of a specified person or to bearer'. In simple terms it is a cheque, similar in form to the personal cheque book.

Usually a bill of exchange is payable at 'sight' and is normally referred to as a 'sight draft'. This means that the bank will not release the documents to the buyer until the buyer has paid for the goods. The buyer will not be allowed to collect the goods until he is able to present the documents. There is, therefore, a clear element of security.

DOCUMENTARY LETTERS OF CREDIT

A documentary letter of credit is issued to the exporter by a bank. The bank promises to pay the exporter providing all the conditions laid down in the credit are met.

The safest letter of credit is an irrevocable letter of credit confirmed by a UK bank.

A letter of credit is only safe when all the conditions are met. This is by no means being achieved. SITPRO reported in the *Institute of Credit Management Magazine* (March 1990) that because exporters do not comply with the details of the letter of credit, i.e. they overlook details, 'an average exporter is still losing over 20% of invoice value on letter of credit business and that is on top of bank fees payable when nothing goes wrong'. They estimate that 'over the country at large, the success rate at first presentation of documents is probably not much over 20%'.

The Midland Bank tries to put this right by issuing a checklist to help exporters. The list contains 15 hints on how to get it right first time.

(1) Does it state that it is subject to UCP? (UCP is the Uniform Customs and Practice for documentary credits. It sets out the conditions under which bankers issue and act on commercial credits. The International Chamber of Commerce can advise.)

(2) Is it irrevocable, preferably with the added confirmation of the advising bank?

(3) Are the terms of settlement clearly expressed and satisfactory?

(4) Where is it available? If it does not provide for settlement in your own country, payment for your goods may be delayed and possibly your security of payment reduced.

(5) Does it describe correctly the goods, their weight, quantity, etc.?

(6) Are there any spelling errors? If there are, they should be taken up immediately with the advising bank. Any needed amendments of the credit should then be communicated to your buyers.

(7) Are there any ambiguities? If there is anything in the credit which is not absolutely clear or which may be interpreted in more than one way take it up with the advising bank.

(8) Are the terms for despatch of the goods, e.g. FOB, CIF, etc., as agreed in your sales contract?

(9) Are all the transport details correctly stated, such as place and time of dispatch, the destination, the method of carriage?

(10) Are part shipments and transhipments allowed?

(11) Does it call for the correct transport documents for the method of carriage to be employed?

(12) Does it require any special declarations, of certification of documents, including references to export or import licences?

(13) Can you comply with the credit terms particularly as regards despatch and presentation time limits and documents stipulated, bearing in mind possible difficulties and delays in obtaining outside certifications?

(14) If the credit stipulates that certain documents are to be sent direct to a third party will you be able to provide the paying bank with documentary evidence that this has been done?

(15) Who pays the bank's charges? If you do, are they clearly stated?

The Midland Bank completed a major study with SITPRO back in the 1980s. A number of errors associated with letters of credit were found, and a list of the most common errors was produced. These errors are still occurring. In the survey 25% of documents were rejected for the following three reasons:

(1) The letter of credit had expired.

(2) The documents were presented after the period stipulated in the letter of credit.

(3) The shipment was late.

The following are some of the other common discrepancies found when presenting documents to the bank:

- There was a claused (i.e. unclean or dirty) shipping document.
- A charter party bill of lading was used when the letter of credit called for on-board shipment.
- The goods were shipped on deck when it was not permitted.
- An insurance document of a type other than that required by the letter of credit was presented.

- The insurance risks covered were not as specified in the letter of credit.
- The insurance cover was expressed in a currency other than that of the letter of credit.
- The goods were underinsured.
- The insurance was not effective from the date of shipment of dispatch.

In addition, the bank found that documents were often inconsistent with one another in the following ways:

- The description (or spelling) of goods on invoice(s) differed from that in the letter of credit.
- The weights differed between export documents.
- The amounts of value shown on the invoice(s) and bill of exchange (draft) differed.
- The marks and numbers differed between documents.
- The drawing was for less than the letter of credit amount (when part shipments were not permitted).
- The letter of credit was exceeded by the value of the order.
- The bill of lading did not show evidence whether freight was paid or not.
- The shipment was short.
- There was an absence of document(s) called for in the documentary letter of credit.
- The bill of exchange (draft) was drawn on the wrong party.
- The bill of exchange (draft) was payable on an indeterminable date.
- The bills of lading, insurance or bill of exchange (draft) were not endorsed correctly.
- The copy of the freight account was not attached (when called for by documentary letter of credit).
- There was an absence of signatures of witnessings, where required, on documents presented.
- Facsimile signatures were used when not allowed.

- There was an absence of 'on board' notation on bills of lading.
- There was an absence of endorsement on documents, e.g. bills of lading, insurance documents.

SITPRO cites banks as not always having an adequate number of trained staff to deal with the problems. The fact that agents who are asked to produce documents are not fully instructed does not help the exporter or the banks.

Another aspect of the exporting picture is that much of the finance comes in the form of bank overdrafts. SITPRO points to the time it takes banks to transfer money into exporters' accounts even though they possess the ability to transfer the money in seconds.

CONCLUSION

There is no substitute for having experienced people check each detail to make sure that paperwork is spot on. Even when the details are absolutely correct there are still lots of other things that can go wrong. It just seems like an awful waste of everyone's time, when the whole business of manufacturing products or offering services is let down by sloppy paperwork.

11.3 Terms and documents of transport

TERMS

The International Chamber of Commerce publishes a list of all the terms. The most widely used are as follows:

Ex-works The overseas buyer collects the goods from the factory gate and is responsible for them from there on.
FAS (free alongside ship) The price includes the cost of delivery to the docks.
FOB (free on board) The price includes loading on board. It does not include air or sea freight or insurance.
CIF (cost, insurance and freight) The price covers the cost

of loading aboard ship, freight and insurance, to the point of delivery, usually the buyer's port.

C + F (cost and freight)   The price covers all charges, except insurance to port of destination.

CIP (freight carriage and insurance paid)   The price covers all charges to a named destination.

DOCUMENTS

A range of documents is shown in Figures 11.4–11.7. The following selection provides a flavour of what is involved in export documentation.

Bill of lading

The Institute of Freight Forwarders lists a number of different types of bills of lading – Through Bill of Lading, Combined Transport Bill of Lading, Negotiable FIATA Combined Transport Bill of Lading and Transhipment Bill of Lading.

A bill of lading (Figure 11.4) is the most common transport document for transporting goods to countries outside Europe and the United States. The bill of lading provides:

- evidence that there is a contract between either the exporter or the importer and a shipping company to transport the goods by sea;
- receipt for goods shipped;
- for a transfer of ownership of the goods.

Probably the flavour and extent of what is involved in transporting goods overseas can be seen in the terms and conditions of a bill of lading.

The air waybill

With one important exception the air waybill (Figure 11.5) is the air equivalent of the bill of lading. It is not a document of title.

Figure 11.4 Bill of lading.

The single administration document (SAD)

The single administration document for exporting and importing
within the European Community and EFTA was introduced
to replace a large cumbersome list required by each country's
regulations.

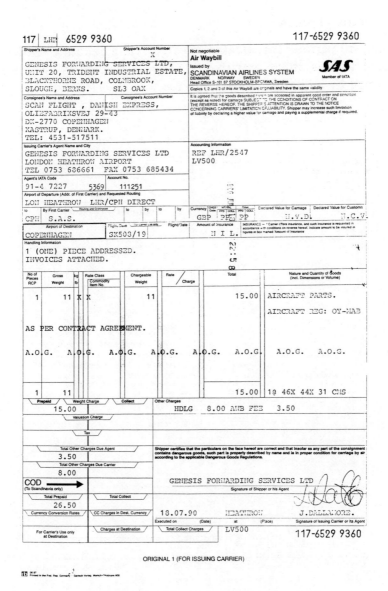

Figure 11.5 Air waybill.

There are eight copies of the document. They are used for customs and excise declarations at the country of departure and entry and at the country of final destination, and there is a copy for the exporter or agent and the importer.

Certificates of origin

There are various certificates of origin. The example shown in Figure 11.6 is an EC certificate. The certificate is issued and stamped by a chamber of commerce.

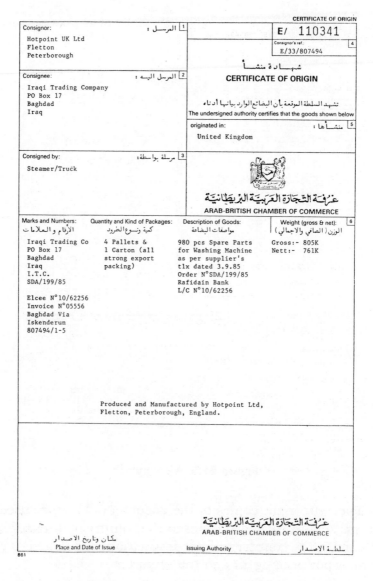

Figure 11.6 Certificate of origin.

Certificate of insurance

An insurance certificate insures goods against loss or damage (see Figure 11.7).

Exporter BRITISH TEXTILES LTD OLD MILL ROAD BRADFORD		**CERTIFICATE OF INSURANCE**	
		Ins. Cert. No: L/A 57329	Exporters Ref: 432/612/9/A
		Code No. 66/AA/ 4632	Agents Ref: FX1-397

This is to certify that

BRITISH TEXTILES LTD

have been issued with an Open Policy and this certificate conveys all rights of the policy (for the purpose of collecting any loss or claim) as fully as if the property were covered by a special policy direct to the holder of this certificate but if the destination of the goods is outside the United Kingdom this certificate may require to be stamped within a given period in order to comply with the laws of the country of destination. Notwithstanding the description of the voyage stated herein, provided the goods are at the risk of the Assured this insurance shall attach from the time of leaving the warehouse, premises or place of storage in the interior.

Norwich Union Fire Insurance Society Ltd. Maritime Insurance Company Ltd.

NORWICH UNION HOUSE,
51/54 FENCHURCH STREET, LONDON EC3M 3LA

Vessel ELLEN	Port of Loading FELIXSTOWE	Insured Value (State Currency) £3421
Port of Discharge AUCKLAND	Final Destination	GBP THREE THOUSAND FOUR HUNDRED & TWENTY ONE POUNDS. so valued

Marks, Nos./Container No.	No. and Kind of Packages	Description of Goods
AC 984 AUCKLAND NOS 1-30		30 CASES TEXTILE PIECE GOODS

IMPORTANT

PROCEDURE IN THE EVENT OF LOSS OR DAMAGE FOR WHICH UNDERWRITERS MAY BE LIABLE

LIABILITY OF CARRIERS, BAILEES OR OTHER THIRD PARTIES

It is the duty of the Assured and their Agents, in all cases, to take such measures as may be reasonable for the purpose of averting or minimising a loss and to ensure that all rights against Carriers, Bailees or other third parties are properly preserved and exercised. In particular, the Assured or their Agents are required:-

1 To claim immediately on the Carriers, Port Authorities or other Bailees for any missing packages.
2 In no circumstances except under written protest, to give clean receipts where goods are in doubtful condition
3 When delivery is made by Container to ensure that the Container and its seals are examined immediately by their responsible official. If the Container is delivered damaged or with seals broken or missing or with seals other than as stated in the shipping documents, to clause the delivery receipt accordingly and retain all defective or irregular seals for subsequent identification
4 To apply immediately for survey by Carriers or other Bailees Representatives if any loss or damage be apparent and claim on the Carriers or other Bailees for any actual loss or damage found at such survey
5 To give notice in writing to the Carriers or other Bailees within three days of delivery if the loss or damage was not apparent at the time of taking delivery
NOTE - The Consignees or their Agents are recommended to make themselves familiar with the regulations of the Port Authorities at the port of discharge

SURVEY AND CLAIM SETTLEMENT

In the event of loss or damage which may involve a claim under this insurance, immediate notice of such loss or damage should be given to and a Survey Report obtained from the Office or Agent nominated herein. In the event of any claim arising under this insurance, request for settlement should be made to the Office or Agent nominated herein

DOCUMENTATION OF CLAIMS

To enable claims to be dealt with promptly, the Assured or their Agents are advised to submit all available supporting documents without delay including when applicable :-
1 Original policy or certificate of insurance
2 Original or copy shipping invoices together with shipping specification and/or weight notes
3 Original Bill of Lading and/or other contract of carriage
4 Survey report or other documentary evidence to show the extent of the loss or damage
5 Landing account and weight notes at final destination
6 Correspondence exchanged with the Carriers and other Parties regarding their liability for the loss or damage

CONDITIONS

Subject to the current Institute Cargo Clauses (A) and/or AIR (as applicable). Subject to Institute Replacement Clause (as applicable). Notwithstanding anything to the contrary contained herein this insurance covers War and Strikes Risks in accordance with the current Institute War and Strikes Clauses which are deemed to be attached to and to form part of this certificate.

SURVEY CLAUSE

In the event of loss or damage which may give rise to a claim under this certificate, notice must be given immediately to the undernoted agent/s so that he/they may appoint a Surveyor if he/they so desire.

Agents at .... AUCKLAND .... are NORWICH WINTERTHUR INSURANCE
(NZ) LTD   QUEEN STREET   AUCKLAND

CLAIMS

In the event of a claim arising under this Certificate it is agreed that it shall be settled in accordance with English law and Custom and shall be so settled

in LXXXXXX .... AUCKLAND ....
by .... AS ABOVE ....

	BRITISH TEXTILES LTD
(signature) N.T. Veukin Marine Underwriter and Manager	Dated 30 MARCH 1990

MARD191-303-Feb90   The original certificate must be produced when claim is made and must be surrendered on payment

Figure 11.7 Certificate of insurance.

11.4 Summary

- Check sources of information.
- Cross-check information.
- The method of payment should depend on how well you know the customer.
- Check and recheck the detail of the documents of payment and transport.

The Help Industry

Almost all companies that fail do so because of mismanagement. Sometimes the last person to hear about it is the chief executive. For this reason it is necessary to aim seriously at getting to know customers better than they know themselves.

The help industry offers services at various stages of customer development. The main participants are:

- management consultants
- credit reference agencies
- insurance companies
- factors
- accountants
- debt collectors/solicitors.

12.1 Management consultants

Most companies that call in consultants are already successful. They look to consultants for advice to sustain their success. They are called in for a variety of reasons:

- To review, overall or specifically.
- To promote a management view, the company, change, etc.
- To improve performance.
- To develop policy, a product, a market, etc.
- To provide a second opinion.
- To train management/workforce.

Consultants have been called in to review one aspect, only to find that improvements are needed elsewhere. Subsequently the terms of reference are changed. Also things may not always be as they appear.

> I remember being called in by one blue chip company where apparent terms of reference covered credit management but I was specifically asked to report to the chief executive on the general ability of management throughout the company.

The two main points to look for when choosing a consultant are:

(1) Choose an expert in the area under review (not necessarily with experience in the same industrial sector, since a new viewpoint can be refreshingly direct).

(2) Meet the people who will actually do the work before making a final decision.

To get the best out of them, keep in constant contact. They are hired for their knowledge – not their ability to write long reports.

12.2 Credit reference agencies

These agencies come in different forms, from the small company that will send three years' annual accounts through the post within 48 hours, to the on-line agencies where the information is supplied on the spot by data link-up. Some offer their own comments on the accounts.

The Institute of Credit Management carries a list which is by no means complete but which is being updated all the time. Other sources that will pin down the agencies are other credit people and trade contacts. Charges vary. It is worth while shopping around.

12.3 Insurance

It is possible to insure all or part of the sales ledger, individual accounts or contracts. The ICM can again help with this information. Generally insurers will insure up to 80% or 90% of the debt. They will require details to be supplied on their forms each month.

12.4 Factors

The principle is that, in return for a fee, factors will pay invoices immediately up to an agreed percentage of the sales ledger.

For example, the agreement may be that they will pay 80% of all invoices immediately, less their fee of, say, 1½% of the invoice total. Contracts are signed initially for one year.

The theory is that the company receives an immediate injection of cash, to support its cashflow.

There are a number of points to bear in mind:

(1) The invoices pass out of the company's hands and debts are collected by the factor.

   (a) Customers will be contacted by the factor whose culture may be different and this may or may not be an advantage.
   (b) If the factor fails to collect the debts within a certain time, say 60 days, the debts revert back to the company.

(2) There may be no saving at all in administration, since any time saved on cash collection may be lost in checking the factor's paperwork and in staying in contact with the factor. Contact becomes cumbersome if staff turnover is high.

(3) Getting the invoices paid immediately may not be so easy in practice. The following sequence may occur:

(a) They are dispatched to the factor once a week.

(b) The factor checks the invoices.

(c) The factor then raises a cheque or pays direct to the company's bank.

This routine may take weeks.

(4) In practice a company only gets the benefit of the 'up front' payment once – the first time.

(5) An alternative may be to rely on a bank overdraft since this can be paid back as the funds become available. Factors are normally subsidiaries of banks.

12.5 Accountancy firms

Good accountants save money.
A few points to bear in mind about accountants:

(1) Accountants make a living by manipulating figures and interpreting rules which they are largely responsible for creating.

(2) Accountancy is not an exact science and can be pretty creative – take for example the Channel Tunnel Company. In 1989 it made a profit by treating a hole in the ground as an asset.

(3) On the whole accountants are not entrepreneurs. Good accountants run with the company thinking rather than put it in a straitjacket.

(4) Experienced auditors can offer useful advice. This could be treated as add-on value to the customer.

(5) Insolvency practitioners look after terminal and near-terminal companies. From the point of view of the credit manager who may have a say in which firm gets the job each time, it might be useful to review who the fallen firm's auditors were.

12.6 Debt collectors

Debt collectors collect debts, where companies' cash collection methods have failed.

They vary in size and services offered. A commercial solicitor may take a different course than an agent dedicated to a particular trade. It is important to do a check on anyone who even at this late stage is your representative. Would you for instance own up to sending a stinking debt collector together with dead rats in each coat pocket into a chain store in London's West End to hang about the perfume counter?

Instructions to debt collectors should be clear and simple. What you do not want is to tie up credit people constantly with this end of the market.

Credit people will not learn how to collect cash by attending courts or creditors' meetings, although it might be a good idea to attend one court session or creditors' meeting, if only to see that an effective cash collection effort can save customers this terrible ordeal. Take this example.

> The creditors' meeting was fixed for a date in the second week of my new appointment.
>
> There were some 300 present. Whispers of shady dealings were circulating before the meeting started. There was even talk about the fraud squad being in the audience.
>
> The failed businessman accompanied by his solicitor and accountant sat miserably at a head table, a bit bewildered by the strength of the attendance.
>
> I had the unenviable task of serving the wretch with a writ. I stood up and approached the head table. The general buzz died a little as I said my bit. The front rows began to relate the incident.
>
> Proceedings had just passed the introduction stages, when the first of the planted creditors' representatives rose and started to harangue the debtor. Words like 'fraud', and 'liar' were followed by more loud accusations of overseas bank accounts (with numbers) and dastardly deeds of products being removed in the dead of night. House of Commons type choruses drowned out the debtor's accountant's excuses.

At the end the wretch had cowered (almost too professionally for some of the creditors) so much that he was barely visible behind the table.

The fraud squad were certainly interested. However, there was no arrest. The debtor later skipped the country.

Years have passed since. But the fraud squad are still interested. Only a few years ago I had a policeman call at my door just to confirm that I was still alive and on the witness list.

12.7 Summary

- Consultants and credit references agents help improve knowledge.
- Insurance is a price to pay for possible failure.
- Look hard before factoring.
- Get the most out of accountants; they charge enough.
- Allow debt collectors to deal with the courts.

PART III

Marketing Strategy Delivered through Credit Management

Management Information

The marketplace is more interested in the satisfaction a product gives it, the product quality and the customer service than in company financial comparison figures between years.

These areas are not as easy to monitor and get right as, say, financial comparisons. The tendency is to become more expert in the easier areas. Therefore, there is a tradition in UK companies of looking at the 'figures' rather than the market.

This results in innovators playing second fiddle when they should be leading the orchestra. Management information should, in the main, feature the market. What message does the company give the market?

13.1 Company message

Some companies project themselves into the market via a single focused message. The message gives a clear indication to customers and staff. IBM's message is 'IBM means service'; British Rail's is 'We're getting there'; British Airways' is 'The world's favourite airline'. The company should be able to deliver the message. The workforce must possess the will to achieve the aim.

13.2 Marketing information

In the main, marketing decisions are based on a range of information that is a mixture of verbal executive and expert opinion, rumour, guesswork and some facts.

Therefore, it should come as a pleasant surprise to marketing people to learn that an effective credit department can fill in vital gaps in market knowledge, and especially in how the company responds to specific customer needs.

The marketing information an effective credit department can get comes direct from the customers. It can demonstrate how to hold on to current customers. And recent surveys are now upgrading the value of keeping customers as against the effort and cost of winning new ones.

In Chapter 10, a suggested system is described to enable the company to respond to customers. This particular system produces accurate information capable of being used by marketing people. It is also capable of expansion. It can then be computerized. And with some fine tuning it can be focused on marketing requirements. A larger management/marketing information system could encompass the entire company personnel, all product lines, product and service quality.

Response times to customer needs by the credit department through customer after-sales service can reinforce the marketing message and at the same time deliver marketing strategy.

13.3 Information on competitors

The main types of management information that it is possible to get on competitors are financial, structural, workrate and behavioural.

(1) Financial information may be in the public domain. It may be straightforward. For instance, comparisons on DSO, profitablity, etc., on a company in one industry sector are genuine. However, it is not normally that simple, although we tend to believe it is. For example, if your company manufactures computers for the UK market, how do you genuinely compare your DSO with a global exporter where the terms of payment are different? Basically you have to take a view and keep monitoring it.

(2) Structural comparisons in the same industry are easier to make. For example, if as a credit manager you answer to a board director and your main competitor answers to a lesser manager, your flatter management structure should give you an advantage. The flatter the management structure the more chance the innovator has got. Flatter management structures can normally change faster, are fitter and more integrated than managements where a ladder of line managers dilutes operational response times to the market.

(3) Workrate of competitors may be easier to get than is realized. In terms of credit management you could arrive at the times your competitors took to administer their workloads if you knew, e.g., how many invoices they produced, cheques they received, and number of personnel involved. You can keep building on this information.

(4) Behavioural patterns and attitudes to customers, management, workforce and to life in general can give clues to what competitors might be capable of achieving, at your expense.

There are other sources such as the media, customers (yours and theirs) and trade organizations.

13.4 Internal information

Most management information is internally generated, whereas products produced by a company are for the outside marketplace. Therefore, it makes sense to focus management's attention on how the internal information is comparing with the generalities and specifics of the outside marketplace. In particular, managers need to get a grasp on how customers are responding to the company's products and service.

13.5 Credit management information

Most information on credit management reports contains a link to customers in the form of sales information (debts) and how customers respond to credit management's collection efforts (aged debts).

Most companies with computerized systems will produce a sales ledger (debtors) aged listing. From this report the credit department is able to present a continuing regular picture on customers' accounts and cash collection. The specimen report (see Figure 13.1), sales outstanding aged analysis, is a basic three-line report each month which is supported by two further reports for other managers who want to get a better flavour of the way the cash collection effort is doing. These further reports are the sales outstanding aged analysis exception report, which looks more closely at the six largest overdue customers' accounts in more detail (see Figure 13.2), and the query summary/customer feedback report, which gives more detail on the ongoing query position (see Figure 10.3).

These three credit management reports give an accurate picture of how the credit department performs from month to month. Part II has demonstrated how the credit department keeps up-to-the-minute management information.

13.6 Timing of management information

A market-orientated company will tend to produce information quickly, as events occur. This benefits both the company and the customers. For example, dispatching invoices on the same day as the product is delivered enables customers to tie up the documents as they arrive. The paperwork does not get filed in the pending tray and so the chances of it going astray are reduced.

Another example would be customers' statements. If these are produced on the last day of the month rather than two weeks later they stand a better chance of being actioned by customers at an earlier stage. Obviously statements are not so important in the computerized environment. But they can be used as an early reminder to those customers who find them useful.

Some companies run a thirteenth sales and accounting period each year. This means that company people must achieve one more target than most companies. Until all customers see

Period _____

Month	Total	Current Terms			Total Current	Days Overdue			
		Norm	60	Misc.		1/30	31/60	61/90	90+
April									
May									
June									
July									
Aug									
Sept									
Oct									
Nov									
Dec									
Jan									
Feb									
Mar									

Month	Actual Sales	DSO		% of days Overdue	Collection Index %	Queries		Cumulative Bad Debts
		Actual	Plan			No	Amount	
Mar								
Apr								
May								
June								
Jul								
Aug								
Sept								
Oct								
Nov								
Dec								
Jan								
Feb								
Mar								

Month	3-Month Forecast		Query Forecast		Doubtful Debts	Comment
	DSO	S/L Bal	Amount	DSO		
Mar						
Apr						
May						
June						
July						
Aug						
Sept						
Oct						
Nov						
Dec						
Jan						
Feb						
Mar						

See text for notes on report calculations and on terms used.

Figure 13.1 Sales outstanding aged analysis specimen report.

The six largest overdue accounts, overdue by more than 30 days. Period									
Name and Location	Last 12 Months	Total Due		Amounts Overdue				Credit Limit
		Prior	This	31/ 60	61/ 90	90/ 120	120+	
		Report						

COMMENTS   Why overdue, action taken, basis for extending credit

1

2

3

4

5

6

Figure 13.2 Sales outstanding aged analysis exception report.

the cashflow benefits of paying invoices on weekly cheque runs, instead of once a month, credit departments that collect cash thirteen times a year are put under extra pressures. This is the price they pay for being out of step with the customers.

13.7 Sales and cashflow forecasts

Sales and cashflow forecasts are the daily and monthly operational measurements of how a company is progressing. They are the financial plans on which a company hopes to achieve its aims. They should be understood by all managers (if not the whole workforce).

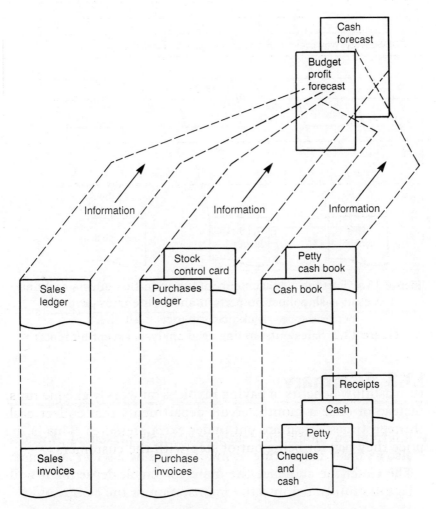

Figure 13.3 Routes of information that affect the cashflow forecast: from primary documentation to management information.

The credit manager is responsible more than any other manager for the top lines of the cashflow and for this reason should be fully involved in disussing its make-up.

Figures 13.3 and 13.4 show some of the routes of information that directly affect the cashflow forecast.

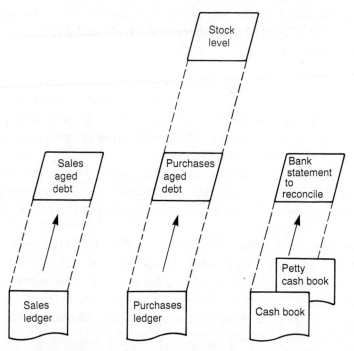

Figure 13.4 Further management information that affects cashflow forecast: cash collection performance; purchases payment performance; stock performance; cash check.

13.8 Summary

- Information should be clearly and simply presented. If it can also be made interesting, it may be read by a wider audience. The wider the audience the more the credit department will become integrated into the mainstream of the company.

Management Control

Workflow and the resources to cope with it must be managed. It is not good enough just to turn up and 'get on with it'.

To achieve company targets, quantity, quality and timing must be carefully planned. The credit management team must see where they fit in the process.

In Figure 14.1, where the initial order is assessed by the proprietor, the credit function commences at the invoice stage. The chart shows where the proprietor expects the credit person to take over.

In Figure 14.2 the directors and sales staff take the orders, using either their local area knowledge or relying on their credit management procedures. The credit people were able to influence the process by persuading suppliers to send in their invoices earlier. This enabled the credit team to plan an improvement in DSO of 12 days.

As the company expands, lines of communication might become more difficult to maintain. Individual roles may seem to be making less of a contribution. The credit team may be split into various tasks and specialization may reduce their overall and general knowledge of how the company operates.

The credit department is itself a fairly specialized function. Further specialization by personnel tends to dilute its influence in keeping in touch with the mainstream company activities. Covering these specialist positions in their absence becomes difficult. It is far easier to manage a department when all the members are performing comparable tasks. Each member's progress can be monitored against the background of the others. Management planning can be served better in a department of 10 by having 9 other potential credit managers.

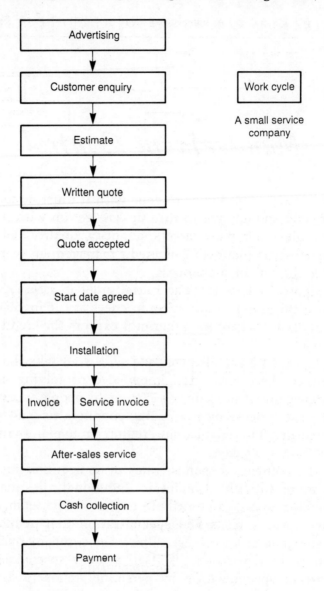

Figure 14.1 Initial order assessed by proprietor.

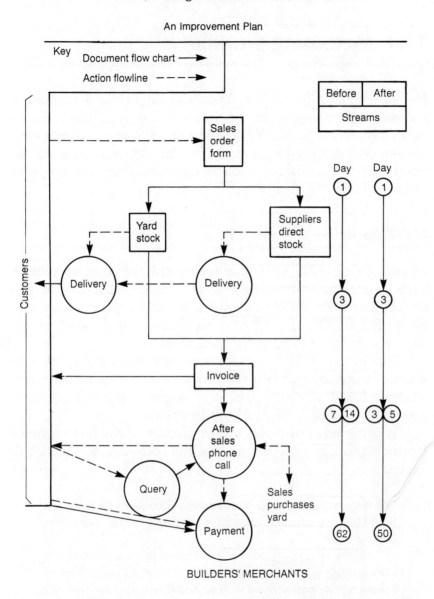

An Improvement Plan

Key
Document flow chart ⟶
Action flowline − − − ⟶

Figure 14.2 Action/document flow chart. (1) Before stream – 62 days from sales order to payment. (2) After stream – 50 days from sales order to payment. (3) Process speeded up by (a) dispatching yard stock invoices on the same day as delivery and (b) chasing suppliers to send their invoices in earlier.

14.1 Measuring workflow

Measure what is important. The most important document in a credit department is an invoice. It is not a difficult task to verify how many invoices are produced each month, since each invoice is numbered sequentially. The invoice produces the other routine documents, such as statements, credit notes, customer queries and cheques.

NUMBERS

By associating the number of invoices with the other documents each month, an average paperflow for the month can be predicted. The average time taken to clear this paperwork can also be predicted. The last 12 months' figures can be used as the basis for the next 12 months' prediction.

The number of live accounts each month can also be predicted and allocated to the credit team for cash collection. The number of contacts needed to secure payment from these accounts can also be worked out in advance.

It sometimes surprises senior managers who haven't given it much thought how far out the numbers can be. Take this example.

> The financial director of a newspaper company told me that his 15,000 live accounts were being looked after by seven credit people.
>
> These seven personnel were responsible for cash collection, cash allocation and answering customers' queries. None had any formal credit management training and three were new recruits. The DSO was given as about 60 days.
>
> An initial investigation revealed that the number of live accounts was 5000. Since some of these customers had more than one account, the number of customers fell to 4000. About 20% of the team's time was spent in correspondence with debt collectors. The DSO was 70 days against the average for the industry of 49. About one-third of all overdue accounts were

for sums of £100 or less. The company turnover was £30 million.

To be fair to the director it is not uncommon for directors to be wildly out. Their priorities may lie elsewhere. However, his interest was awakened when we went through some of the implications, especially when we hit on how much he could improve cashflow.

Taking a bank borrowing interest rate of, say, 13%, and assuming that the department could, with the additional help of two experienced credit people, together with a refocusing of objectives, reduce the DSO to the industry average, he could:

- save bank interest of £205,000 each year;
- plus an increase in cashflow of £1,930,000;
- or a cashflow improvement of £2,135,000 in the first year.

14.2 Quality

If more care is taken at the order processing and invoice stages to get it right first time, it may take longer initially to process the orders and paperwork. But each mistake at these stages causes delays later on. If customers can take for granted that the invoices they receive are correct all the time, this encourages them to process them quickly.

To maintain quality, each individual team member must be monitored closely each month. This demonstrates to the individual that their work is being appreciated and that managers are actually interested in what they do. Individuals like to know where they stand and how managers feel about their performance.

Quality can be judged in a number of ways. Invoice batches can be traced back to the individual at input stage and cheques traced to the cash allocator. The quality of the after-sales service calls and cash collection can be judged by the success rate and margin notes, plus the attitude towards customers, other departments and colleagues.

14.3 Timing

There are about 21 working days in a normal (five day working week) month. Some companies work at crisis management pace all month. This may be because one department is not being monitored tightly enough. Take the following example.

> A company in the medical instrument industry sector pushed through 75% of its sales in the last three days of the month.
>
> This had obvious dire consequences for the cash collection, as customers would receive the invoices in the following month and therefore pay out in the next month (the third month).
>
> Further investigation revealed that 5% of sales were actually made in the first few days of the following month. The credit manager was fighting a losing battle.
>
> The sales director acted very positively to the news. The obvious question of what happened on the other 18 days was explored by the sales team. More planning resulted.
>
> The company became so successful that it bought up its main overseas competitor within the year.

Traditionally, some companies produce their 'cheque run' at the end of the month or the start of the following month. Those companies that stick to this procedure in the mistaken idea that it is prudent 'housekeeping' will find lenders, like bank managers, a bit concerned. The bank manager likes to see a steady cashflow throughout the month. He is not amused by surprises, and large outflows of cash are not seen in business planning circles as good planning. The credit manager, who is also a lender, has to contend with a further challenge. Cheque runs are not known for getting pride of place in the end-of-month documentation.

A sometimes irritating tendency in workload timing from the credit team's side is that while sales are allowed up to the last minute of the last day of the month (with the subsequent documentation being produced after the deadline), cash collected is only counted if it reaches the company's credit department before the deadline (even if sometimes a credit person is holding the cash before the deadline). Take the following example.

A London, West End company in the entertainment industry got into the habit of collecting end-of-month cheques following several disruptions to the mail service.

In this particular month the credit people were getting more than the usual buzz. It looked like the department would beat all the company records for cash collection – by an unbelievable margin. This was also going to be a good show for the newly appointed credit manager.

Hunting parties were dispatched all across the country. As each cheque was collected the cheque collector would telephone the office with the amount of the cheque.

At 4.45 p.m. the largest cash collector reported from a mainline terminal that his train had been delayed and that there was no underground service. He would take a taxi. Without this cheque the unbelievable would be just that – unbelievable. Looking out of the window, personnel could see blocked streets of traffic due to the movement of people out of the underground. Apprehension was beginning to creep into the celebratory mood.

The deadline of 5.30 p.m. came and went. The safe was locked. Still, everyone waited. At 5.50 p.m. the hot, exhausted wretch arrived panting. He'd run the last few miles. The credit manager went to see his director in an effort to make some sense of the day and to revive the low spirits of his disappointed team. He was unsuccessful.

So a future good campfire yarn died a sad fate.

14.4 Summary

- Management control means getting to grips with all aspects of the business. Getting the detail right is all important. It is the detail that impresses the customers, both inside and outside the company.

Human Resources

15.1 Reports and surveys

(1) A report conducted by the Henley Management College in 1989 for a client – Lunchen Vouchers – asked the question,

'What do you want from a job?'

The answers were:

- job training and development
- recognition of employees' contribution
- opportunity to be innovative
- further education
- better health care
- better management

(2) Back in 1985 in the National Institute of Economic and Social Research's review was a study on productivity of 25 British and 20 West German engineering companies.

The overall view of the report that followed the review found that British managers were complacent, lacked skill, showed too many examples of management inertia, were inadequately organized and had a general couldn't care less attitude.

The Germans had higher qualifications from management down to the shop floor. British salespeople had little or no technical background. In Britain machines were frequently abused and maintenance procedures ignored.

The report noted that in one British firm it took 13 years to agree manning levels for new machines. Also noted was the decrease in the number of trainees under the supervision of the Engineering Industry Training Board over the years from 1967 (28,000) to 1983 (9000).

One German company with plants in both countries said that while output was the same in Britain, when 'the machine broke down there was no one to repair it'.

(3) *The Making of Managers*, a National Economic Development Council publication/report in association with the British Institute of Management, says that compared with managers in Japan, France and West Germany (i.e. preunification), British managers are amateurs.

British managers, the report continues, are less well educated and trained and there are too many accountants. Half of the 3,300,000 managers have no formal training or help in career development.

(4) *Mental Health at Work*, a report by Dr Graham Lucas of King's College Hospital, London, reports that mental illness or emotional problems can be blamed for nearly 40% of absenteeism at work caused by overpromotion or resentment at failure to be promoted, too much or too little work, relocation, change in work environment or of colleagues, change in the nature and style of management, role conflict or ambiguity, irregular or long hours, lack of autonomy, machine-based monotonous work, perceived hazards such as infection and actual or potential violence.

Also underlined was how the design of the workplace and working procedures can affect physical and mental health.

The three main aspects of mental health at work are:

- recognition
- intervention
- resettlement

Uncertainty, the report finds, is the most common cause of anxiety.

(5) The CBI survey of 343 British companies (1987) showed that manual workers lost 4% (9 days) of working time the previous year through being ill. Non-manual workers lost

2.2% (or 5 days) through being ill. Sickness and absenteeism increased with the size of the company.

The chairman of the BMA's Occupational Health Committee, Dr William Dixon, indicates that lots of decisions by employees at 7.30 a.m. about going to work with a cold, ankle injury, etc., will be determined by how they feel about their boss, colleagues and company.

One company in South Wales introduced a rule that people going sick had to ring up themselves. Absenteeism was cut to 2%. Borderline cases tended to get someone else to ring up, while those who were really ill couldn't care who they spoke to.

Firms with high absentee rates suffered because management did not communicate with the workforce, could not be bothered to lay down strict procedures and would not train supervisory staff to deal with the problem.

(6) Lord Young, the then Secretary of State for Trade and Industry, in a speech to the National Economic Development Council in 1988, quoted some more statistics:

'One-third of our middle managers have no training since starting work.'
'Only one-fifth of all our managers have degrees or professional qualifications of any sort, compared with 63% in West Germany and 85% in the USA.'

Postscript: These comments on British management would seem to point loud and clear to a need to have educated and trained managers.

It is sad to reflect on the muddled thinking of some companies who put managers through such valuable courses as Master of Business Administration (MBA) without any clear idea of how to use the managers.

15.2 The manager

Terry Lunn, Personnel Director of Joshua Tetley & Son, wrote in a *Sunday Times* article (May 1989) that 'How people feel about their managers determines what they are prepared to put into the job'.

If these managers are as untrained and uneducated as the reports and surveys indicate, this must surely show itself in the way they treat those they supervise as well as the other resources they manage.

There ought to be a way to recognize excellent managers and promote them. The current recognition seems to rely on the capacity of the company car.

A better way might be to publish the salary of all manager grades along with a points system of service recognition. The service recognition might consist of a points system with points for excellence (innovation, team leadership, performance, etc.), and other merit points for, say, loyalty, educational and training courses attended, languages, etc. Each point earned would receive a monetary bonus. This would indicate to managers and the workforce the board's intention to reward excellence. Obviously the same system would apply to the whole workforce.

The basic assumption that the manager knows best does not always work in reality. The manager is someone who leads and pulls a team together. He relies on the individual expertise of the members of the team and does not always have to be an expert in the individual expert functions. For the same reasons that the chief executive will listen to the other members of the board, the manager must take into account what his workforce wants.

15.3 Team building

A manager's expertise is in getting the most out of his team to achieve the company's strategic aims. A significant part of this ability is, initially, to choose the best possible team.

There is a tendency among managers to pick people for the team because they 'fit in'. 'Fitting in' relates to the image the new team member might create. This may not unfortunately be the same as the ability to deliver. The 'fitting in' philosophy dilutes the team's expertise rather than adds to it.

I remember one night's training at a rugby club where the mood was so opposed to the way the first team was picked that the players threatened to withdraw from the selection process, which in turn meant that the club would not be able to put out a team.

The reason for this revolt was that the selectors would not pick a player for the first team who all the players wanted in the team. The player did not 'fit in' with their image of the club first 15. This was purely because of the snobbish attitude of the selectors towards a particular part of town where the player lived.

The players got their way. And the player who was elevated to the first team became an international, seven games later.

Being in a good team is reward in itself but it is even better if the team is winning. A good team is one where the team members come together in an atmosphere of almost naive enthusiasm that always looks forward to the next challenge. Hallmarks of a good team are tolerance, innovation, back-up and different backgrounds.

15.4 The individual

Nothing moves in business without the will of some individual to make things happen. Having invested time and money in recruiting an individual it is important to look after the investment.

Quite often the individual's perception of the new company does not match the company's high regard it has for itself. This may not be apparent to either party on day one of the association, but the new company member all too quickly develops a veneer to hide frustration.

The following routine is a recipe that should be changed but unfortunately is a part of the business life some new company people must digest.

- The new team member has a five-minute chat with the manager.
- He is then left in the care of either a colleague, or the person who is leaving, or he is left on his own 'to get on with it'.

- After the initial first day in which he is introduced to a range of people, given some company literature to look through, collects his stationery and has a chat with the personnel department, he is then expected 'to get on with it'.

- Perhaps the manager may call him in for a brief chat during the first week.

- If the individual is bright, by the third week he will be hauled over the coals for using his own initiative. Since he will have been left on his own he will have taken all the day-to-day decisions. Some of these decisions or all of them may be spot on. But this need not necessarily be the way the company does things. Therefore, other company people including the line manager may perceive errors where they do not exist.

- The new incumbent soon learns that fitting in with company culture is much more important than getting things right. It will take a very strong-minded character continually to oppose 'the system' and most do not. There is another alternative: he could look for work in a new company. But there is no guarantee that the position would be any different. And in any case changing jobs so frequently would not be smiled upon.

- The pressure to conform does not relieve the individual's frustration for self-expression and innovative thinking. But it does bottle it up. To some extent he finds relief in that he realizes that others are in the same boat – the *Titanic!*

- In some companies the rules, procedures and company management structure produce a culture based more on keeping an old *status quo* pecking order than anything resembling a realistic market-orientated approach. Time-consuming chores, which have more to do with maintaining a flourishing bureaucracy, ensnare creativity. Innovative suggestions are put down to aggressiveness. The individual fails to stand out. The company loses the personal touch. It, therefore, deteriorates into a faceless entity which the individual feels powerless to change. However, change it must.

15.5 Change

Change must be seen to be a clear way forward. It must be seen as benefiting the customers and the workforce. The actual exercise or transition is as important as the the results of change. This is because it must be discussed openly and everyone consulted. It will rely on all the workforce accepting change for it to succeed. Change is often difficult to achieve. The ground must be carefully prepared. There are no short cuts.

Innovation is usually stifled because there are too many people in the way of the ideas going forward to those who are able to see their worth and those who can decide to accept the ideas and support them. In some companies they have apparently solved much of the problem by taking one or more management layers out of the company structure. This results in the board of directors getting closer to the first-level company employee. The workforce will normally see this as a first positive step, though if the workforce were not initially consulted they will feel less inclined to part-own the reasons for the decision. It is, therefore, possible for the board to lose the initiative.

People who do not get *information* cannot take responsibility. Good quality information deserves greater responsibility. By far the most important information is customer information. Up-to-date customer information keeps the company workforce in tune with the marketplace. Customer information:

- changes from day to day, and over the short, medium and long term;
- is a direct line to the marketplace;
- is the most accurate information available;
- is innovative (according to Tom Peters and Robert Waterman, in their book *In Search of Excellence*, some of the most successful companies they came across in their research got their best ideas from customers);
- can be a quality control check.

Any *management information system* that puts the work-force in touch with the customers is going to have an immediate impact on day-to-day company operations. Therefore, in designing a system, it needs to be carefully put together, seen to be fair on the workforce, constantly monitored and action biased (to get results, since without a recognizable results indicator there would be nothing to achieve). And it is the will of the management and the workforce alike to achieve aims and improve performance, that will keep such a system going.

Successful companies will have a good sense of communication, and integration will be tight throughout the organization. However, there are some companies that allow wide gaps between management and workforce thinking, and between aspirations and knowledge of how the company is doing and what each wants.

In one particular company in the music industry the management were discussing closing down the factory because it was losing money, while the workforce were demanding a significant pay rise.

A company in the precision instruments industry sector that had made many of its workforce redundant had increased its computer department personnel by 300% even though there was far less work to monitor.

In a motorcar manufacturer of expensive cars there were the workers who were prepared to drive out of the factory gates like maniacs irrespective of the road conditions, while the marketing management were creating a sense of care and skill as selling points of the product.

As a prelude to introducing the company to a fully integrated customer information system an initial quite natural start could be made by using the credit department to present customer information to company departments. This was demonstrated in Chapter 10.

A further step along the road of planning to deliver corporate aims through the credit department is to organize individual plans for each member of the team (see Table 15.1). This plan would be talked over with individuals. It can grow in detail as both the manager and team member target their objectives more

Table 15.1 Monthly management plan.

Week	Monday	Tuesday	Wednesday	Thursday	Friday

accurately. Any plan should be capable of being achieved. A team meeting once a month would incorporate the overall monthly plan. The agenda would be agreed so that team members can get used to the idea of preparing for the meetings. Topics would be openly discussed and minutes kept. Sometimes it takes a little time for people actually to discuss things out in the open. The more such meetings are supported by senior management the more the personnel and the company will gain. If necessary, the credit manager should be trained to run such meetings.

15.6 Motivation

There is a tendency among some companies in hard times to review headcount with the aim of cutting costs, i.e. personnel. The positive way forward in hard times is to motivate the workforce to do better.

The trouble with the headcount philosophy review as against a rethink of company strategy is that it seems the easiest option at the time. A hire and fire company will not get loyalty from its workforce. In the short term it gives rise to anxiety about imminent security and in the long term makes life for the individual difficult to plan. This can't be good for the company or the individual.

On occasion the headcount philosophy can be totally misguided. Take the following example.

> The MD of a company in the food industry (turnover £20 million) called me in to review his management information systems.
>
> I couldn't help noticing the absence of a credit manager, a DSO figure that was getting worse each month and the sheer volume of work that was being left undone.
>
> The MD hand on heart explained he had made an error of judgement. He had sacked his credit manager, believing quite wrongly that he could save money on salary. His reasoning was that most of his customers had always paid on time and that they would continue to do so.
>
> The credit manager was fired by success.

Motivation is essential to any plan. Constant checking on the current state of affairs during the month by the credit manager shows the personnel that the manager is serious about achieving the targets. Support from the board reinforces this monitoring and appreciation process. Taking a personal interest in the individual is by far the greatest motivator.

There are other aids, like pulling out the occasional winner, the odd appreciation lunch, yearly merit bonus, or simple devices like the barometer chart (see Figure 15.1).

15.7 Training

Any company that takes training seriously will not accept that personnel of whatever level can get away with less than the equivalent of 14 days' training per year.

However, this should only be considered the least that company people should do. Serious contenders for advancement, who should be both encouraged and rewarded, can take further outside training. Courses range all the way up to MBA standard.

It is sometimes said that companies only train people to take higher salaries in competitors' outfits. And this could be the case if the training is not accompanied by other aspects of effective management practices. These practices include advancing the personnel on merit and track record and moving people across departments (i.e. credit people to sales, marketing, logistics, customer service or any other department).

Company personnel ought to realize that companies that train them care about them. Training helps them stay ahead in their field of activity. Training makes them more confident and generally feel better about themselves. If they moved on to a company that did not train its people, the immediate salary increase would in time be devalued as they fell behind in skills and expertise.

A trained workforce will produce better results. This allows the company more leeway in arriving at salary levels and other affordable benefits.

15.8 Summary

- Most surveys on the subject of what employees want out of a job cite job training and development, recognition and opportunity.

- A manager's expertise is in getting the most out of his team.

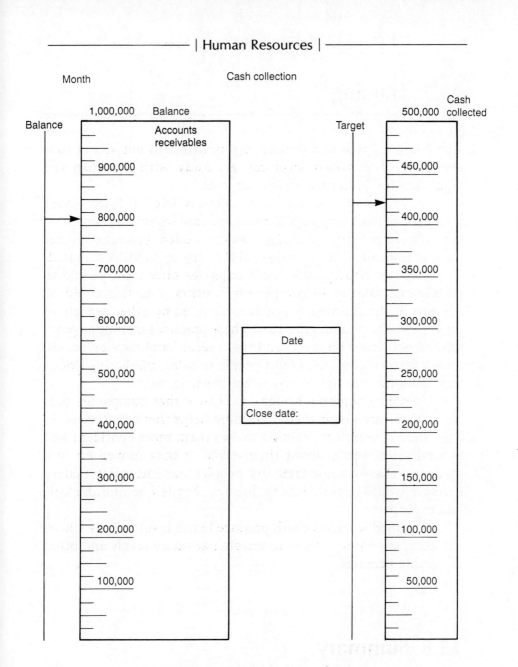

Figure 15.1 Barometer chart.

- Change should be continuous and fair and be based on customers' needs.
- Taking a personal interest in the individual is the best way to motivate.

PART IV

Total Company Integration Delivered through Credit Management

Communication

The quality of communication is the key to all contact with others. The mere fact that there is communication is not good enough.

There are some basic assumptions that ought to be questioned if the quality is to improve.

In common with other company departments that do not physically manufacture products or produce fee income the credit department is an expense, an administration expense, an administration service. Yet the fact that the credit department is a service rarely comes over.

Any service is created to help and give information. Occasionally some service operations may not appear to give this impression. In all good services the quality of the service is closely monitored. Even then the standards depend on how wide the scope of the monitoring is, and where the main focus is placed.

The credit department usually operates within tight restrictive confines. The accumulated knowledge, especially customer information flowing into it each day, is not managed effectively. This is a source of much frustration for credit people. It is easy to see what needs to be done. But it is difficult to do anything, since there is no company mechanism to associate customer needs with company intentions. Defining who the customers are and refocusing the communication effort might be all that is needed to improve the service and give better value for money.

Anyone who has been in a credit department for a few minutes cannot fail to recognize one sort of customer: the customer that pays the invoices. But there is also the one that pays the wages. The customer that operates from within the same company can often be overlooked.

The following tale illustrates the value of recognizing the customer within the company.

> I remember a first date. I needed to carry off an impressive evening.
>
> My company owned a cinema in the heart of London's West End. My staff card allowed me to take a partner to the cinema. I took Jane.
>
> We dined at a little Italian place in theatreland where the owners seem to put on their own stage show. Jane found it refreshing.
>
> As we approached the cinema, I could see a long queue. I hadn't been before, so I was not familiar with the routine. I went up to the uniformed commissionaire at the head of the queue. Putting my staff card out for him to see, I quietly said, 'Staff'.
>
> 'Staff', he repeated, so that the front of the queue could hear. 'This way Sir', ushering us towards the cashier. And then talking to the cashier in the same pitch, 'Staff Miss Morgan, the best seats in the house please'. We then followed the commissionaire who waved us royally into an empty cinema to claim the best seats.
>
> Jane was very impressed.
>
> What a service.

Recognizing the customer all the time can bring its rewards. Salespeople, for example, would not be amused if the credit manager stopped supplying their next call on the day of the call. Salespeople deserve a good service. If the salespeople fail, the company fails too.

But it does not stop there. Here are some other customers to think about:

- *Manufacturing* No company sets out to produce a car that needs to go into the repair yard every month, an alarm clock that goes off 20 minutes late, or a house where the windows occasionally fall out. The sooner they find out when and where they are going wrong the better.

- *Marketing* Compared with other countries in the world we in the UK are not a complaining lot. That is, we complain like hell to our friends about things but not to the manufacturers. Some reasons for this are that we do not like to make waves or to make fools of ourselves in front of others, or we are so relaxed (i.e. lazy) about things that we will accept second best. We cannot export our seconds philosophy overseas. Information about where we are going wrong is needed sooner rather than later.

- *Sales* Some switchboards take minutes to respond to calls. The reason might be very simple. For instance, there is one fault on a certain switchboard that sounds to the customer as if it is ringing, but it has not actually reached the board lights. There is nothing more infuriating to a disappointed customer than to wait for ages for someone to pick up the phone. By the time the customer gets hold of the salesperson the original complaint may be lost in fermenting fountains of issuing forths. Potential customers who cannot get through ring someone else.

16.1 Actively listening

Customers will complain more and more if they feel that the company is taking notice of what they say. If the company is listening to the customers they will be doing something positive about the customers' complaints and getting better at serving the customers. If a company can get customers to monitor its service by encouraging them to communicate freely, the company will have the best possible monitoring device. It is simple, it is direct, it is marketing orientated and easily measured. The most important ingredient to measure in commerce is customer satisfaction. This leads to the ultimate communication goal of getting it right first time.

To accept that when customers complain they are in effect ultimately improving the company service, may not always be an easy pill to swallow in some quarters. Obviously to ignore customers' complaints is to commit commercial suicide.

Some companies take customers' complaints very seriously indeed. IBM salespeople spend part of their training answering customers' complaints before being allowed out to sell. The fact that IBM is by far the largest computer company in the world is not down to chance.

16.2 Communication faults

Most people despise rudeness in others. Yet rudeness is a common communication fault. Its varying degrees often go undetected in departments and individuals within a company. What is missing in the main is the recognition that others' perceptions of the service may be different. In fact, it sometimes looks like there is so little time to get through the daily grind, that thinking about how others feel is beyond some people. Some offences include:

(1) The telephone
    (a) Not answering the telephone on the first or second ring – there is a bad practice of allowing a few rings to give the caller the impression that people are busy.
    (b) Promising to return a call but failing to do so.
    (c) Treating some calls as a nuisance, i.e. wrong time.
    (d) Interrupting and anticipating the caller's remarks.
    (e) Passing the caller over to someone else without knowing whether he can help.

(2) Meetings
    (a) Attending a meeting to get a point across, while showing no interest in anyone else's points.
    (b) Talking to be heard rather than saying anything of value.
    (c) Using superior company position to overtalk and interrupt juniors.
    (d) Arriving unprepared, without having done any work on the issues that will be raised.
    (e) Arriving late, or leaving early.

(3) Demeaning rules and practices
    (a) Separate canteens for different grades or functions.
    (b) Encouraging staff to be deceptive – asking secretaries to lie about whereabouts.
    (c) Putting people down when they make mistakes, rather

than drawing attention to the reasons why and demon-
strating the correct way.

(d) Forgetting people's names or pretending to forget.

(e) Putting down staff in front of customers.

(f) Blaming staff rather than accepting responsibility.

16.3 Messages

A company pursuing market goals while punishing mistakes communicates no advancement to self-motivators. Such a message comes over to the customer in hesitation and autocratic or bureaucratic waves. A decline is almost inevitable. One of the first to notice is the credit manager. In fact a first sign in any company that things are not going well may be when the credit manager starts looking for a job outside the company.

On the other hand, if a company actively encourages the credit manager to keep in close touch with all other functions the chances are that customers are doing the same.

16.4 Summary

- Communication is a basic skill of the credit department. The quality of the communication can be seen as a benchmark for the company.

Promoting Credit Management

Some good reasons for promoting credit management are:

(1) Promote credit management to capture customer information.
  (a) *Marketing information*
    (i) Marginally more accurate marketing information flows into the credit department each day than to the sales department. This information is given willingly by customers to credit people in the normal course of their daily routine.
    (ii) Capturing the information in a structured marketing sense for eventual marketing process would enable the company to react more quickly to the marketplace.
    (iii) In adopting more of a marketing poise, leaning away from financial philosophy, the credit team will receive a more sympathetic hearing from customers, in their main quest for payment of accounts.

  (b) *Quality control*
    (i) Some companies in the United Kingdom sell 'seconds' as a separate product. This encourages the workforce to become sloppy and produce a market for inferior quality goods. These goods are not marketable overseas. Obviously in these cases the internal quality control has failed.
    (ii) Credit management can, through the steps put forward in this book, offer a quality control service to manufacturing and production departments based on customer information. This is the most

direct and accurate quality control source.

(iii) Although it is preferable to produce first-class goods for customers in the first place, nonetheless customers who feel that they have a say in how the goods are produced are more inclined to buy the company's products.

(iv) The process of exchanging information (on product quality) heightens the workforce's awareness of the need to produce quality products and that in order to do this they must strive for individual improvement. This produces a more highly skilled workforce.

(c) *Company integration*

(i) Because the source of the information is from outside the company, and is direct from the people who receive the product/service, it is impartial. The customers will have no axe to grind with particular departments or individuals. They will in fact want the best people to get to the top so that the service improves.

(ii) The information is directed to the people in the company who can best action it. Each such action is monitored. Since all customer information is monitored in an even way, it tends to be more readily accepted by the recipients. Therefore, the will to act upon it is more positive (even though it is largely a criticism brought to their attention by another internal department). This adds to the will or business philosophy of each department, in turn, to accept criticism (in the short term) as part of the general environment of being able to do better in the future (and long term). It is a well-known fact that most people know that they can do better.

(d) *Change*

Keeping all company departments in touch with customers' requirements is closely allying them to the need for change. Customers introduce change into the company continually. Customer information can be used deliberately to create the mood for change in the company.

(e) *Market reserach*

In addition to the market research initiated by the marketing department, with the help of, say, outside agencies, the credit department can play a role. For example, the customers could be asked the same three questions each quarter. These might be vital questions or questions aimed at substantiating marketing department theories.

(f) *Further information systems*

(i) *Customer enquiries* As part of the mechanism of, or in addition to, the customer information systems described in this book, an across-the-board customer enquiry system could be set up. This might be more easily introduced to a company already familiar with an action-biased and customer-orientated outlook. The new customer-enquiry system might incorporate currently used systems or might act alongside them. Its aim might be to produce more accurate marketing information, to analyse customer comments, to produce more information on how the company and its parts respond to customers, or to each other, or to check on any number of different company aspects.

(ii) *Workforce ideas* Customers' ideas have made companies successful in the past, and will continue to do so in the future. The workforce also have ideas. But listening to the workforce is a prerequisite to capturing their ideas. Rewarding them is another.

A system where the immediate supervisor can pinch the idea or squash it will not work. The system must be as impartial as the customer information system. Individual workforce members must get and feel they get a fair hearing. Even if many ideas are unworkable, it is creating the atmosphere in which people will feel comfortable and encouraged to put forward ideas that will produce success.

Such a system or forum for the workforce to air views, ideas and grievances allows them to release bottled-up feelings which normally get in the way of clear thinking and individual commitment. Seeing how a comparable system for customers works would help the workforce to believe in the ability of the company to run a fair system.

(g) *Financial responsibility*

The Institute of Credit Management estimates that cash collectors are responsible for one-third of the assets of British business.

The credit department, like the sales department, is closely monitored. Also like the sales department it is results orientated. Its first target is DSO. This is an easy measurement of how the company is doing, and is seen as such in the sets of operational business ratios used by other companies and the City. So although needing to have a customer-orientated approach to the work, the credit department is not allowed to take its eyes off the goal – DSO.

(2) Promote credit management by promoting credit people. Some of the skills credit management/department people must possess are:

(a) *Communication skills*
   (i) Ability to listen – not to be confused with trying to search for the answer while someone else is talking, or staying silent and not saying anything.
   (ii) Friendly outgoing nature – customers are business partners.
   (iii) Diplomacy – an ambassador of the company.
   (iv) Sympathetic approach – an understanding for others' predicaments, i.e. other departments' mistakes.
   (v) Good negotiator – not argumentative, fair and flexible, thinking long term.

(vi) A liking for others – awareness of others' self-esteem, dignity of the individual.

(vii) Clarity of thought, spoken and written – keeping it simple.

(viii) An enquiring mind – what customers do is important and showing an interest in their business builds their confidence in the company service you offer.

(b) *Motivation skills*

(i) Self-motivated – a built-in bias for action now, not later.

(ii) Absorbs pressure – lives on pressure and concentrates on what is important, serving the individual customer.

(iii) Achieves targets – numerate capabilities.

(iv) Systematic – goes through planned work.

(c) *Coordination skills*

(i) Plans ahead – workflow, timing, projects.

(ii) Interface links – customers, other departments, credit reference agencies, debt collectors.

(d) *Judgement skills*

(i) Decision time all the time – when to do, what to do, and how to do.

(ii) Mistakes – ability to apologize for own and company mistakes and to recover.

(3) Promote credit management by promoting the credit manager.

The credit manager is in constant touch with the whole company operation through the daily routine of dealing with customers. An accurate grasp of customer perception emerges through this contact. This is not generally fully exploited by company management.

Recent research is uncovering more evidence about the cost effectiveness of keeping customers and selling more to them as against finding new customers. The line a customer draws before changing supplier may well be more understood by the credit manager than by other company managers.

The credit manager must be sensitive (to customer

predicaments and errors by other company departments) and a good company organizer and persuader to coordinate the correction of company mistakes that are thrown up by customers. Putting some urgency into getting things done to satisfy customers takes the credit manager out of the more comfortable financial umbrella network, into the hustle and bustle of minute-by-minute marketplace activity. In some respects this isolates him. A certain resilience to accepting the *status quo* results. Credit managers don't normally fight their corner so much as fight for the company and its customers.

The credit manager will have a firm grasp of the financial implications of taking on new customers and dealing with them. He will understand the financial operation plans of sales/budget/profit and cashflow forecasts, and will be heavily involved in cashflow, the company's lifeline.

The credit manager works under similar pressures to the managers of sales, manufacturing, production and distribution departments. These are results orientated, work to deadlines and are easily monitored. Being in regular touch with these departments on a daily basis he is able to appreciate the issues that most concern them.

To exploit the knowledge and skills of the credit manager and credit department's true potential, it is necessary to give the department's activities a higher profile. The credit department needs to be promoted. One way to achieve this is to promote the credit manager.

In these times of global markets more customers are looking for a better service. At the same time companies are sending out messages of intent. These messages ring hollow if the company cannot deliver. And it is a fact that bad news travels faster. If the intent is to give the best possible service to customers, the message ought to be loud, clear and achievable. Putting a customer service director on the board is a good positive step. Also, promoting the person with the best track record in this area will help deliver the intent. The credit manager has first-class credentials.

Index